Using Learning Contracts

*Practical Approaches to
Individualizing and
Structuring Learning*

Malcolm S. Knowles

·☐☐·☐☐·

Using Learning Contracts

Jossey-Bass Publishers

San Francisco   •   London   •   1986

USING LEARNING CONTRACTS
Approaches to Individualizing and Structuring Learning
by Malcolm S. Knowles

Copyright © 1986 by: Jossey-Bass Inc., Publishers
433 California Street
San Francisco, California 94104

&

Jossey-Bass Limited
28 Banner Street
London EC1Y 8QE

Library of Congress Cataloging-in-Publication Data

Knowles, Malcolm Sherperd (date)
    Using learning contracts.

    (The Jossey-Bass higher education series) (The
Jossey-Bass management series)
    Bibliography: p. 249
    Includes index.
    1. Individualized instruction.   2. Performance
contracts in education.   3. Continuing education.
I. Title.   II. Title: Learning contracts.   III. Series.
IV. Series: Jossey-Bass management series.
LB1031.K56   1986   371.3'94   86-45621
ISBN 1-55542-016-8 (alk. paper)

Manufactured in the United States of America

The paper in this book meets the guidelines for
permanence and durability of the Committee on
Production Guidelines for Book Longevity of the
Council on Library Resources.

JACKET DESIGN BY WILLI BAUM

FIRST EDITION

Code 8624

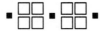

A joint publication in
The Jossey-Bass
Higher Education Series
and
The Jossey-Bass Management Series

Consulting Editors
Human Resources

Leonard Nadler
Zeace Nadler
College Park, Maryland

Contents

Preface

In my fifty years as an adult education practitioner I have begged, borrowed, and stolen many ideas and techniques from other educators, and most of them have improved my practice. But the one that has made the most difference in what I do and has solved the most problems that have plagued me as an educator is the process of contract learning. And I don't even know from whom I stole it. I think it was just an idea that was floating in the air in the mid sixties, and I reached up and grabbed a piece of it and started experimenting.

I started experimenting in my graduate courses at Boston University, first in one or two units of a course, then in special independent study projects, then for whole courses. Magical things started happening. Students began to understand course objectives more clearly and to become committed to them more deeply. Students with widely different learning styles, backgrounds, paces of learning, and other idiosyncrasies began to plan strategies and use resources for learning that took into account their wide range of differences. *Learning became individualized.* I now use learning contracts in almost everything I do (except in giving keynote speeches, which I do as seldom as I can get away with).

As I have traveled around the country (and the world) in the last twenty years conducting workshops in educational institutions, corporations, government agencies, professional societies, health agencies, voluntary organizations, religious institutions, and other social systems, I have been impressed with how rapidly the use of learning contracts has been spreading. I have observed, also, that there is a wide range of differences in the format and quality of these contracts. I believe that providing practitioners with examples of a variety of contracts will result in a general improvement in the quality and effectiveness of contract learning.

Furthermore, people find the contracting process confusing and anxiety-producing when they start using it. Many people have told me that if they had only had some models to look at before they started, they would have been a lot more confident and productive.

The purpose of this book, therefore, is to provide a range of examples of contracts actually developed in a variety of real situations, with brief explanations of the process by which they were developed and monitored. (Throughout the book, my commentary on the contracts appears in a sans serif typeface.) The book is intended to serve as a sourcebook for program administrators in orienting their faculties and human resource development staffs, for instructors in designing their learning experiences, and for learners in constructing their contracts. But it also provides (in Chapter Two) the theoretical rationale for organizing learning this way.

The examples of contracts that form the heart of this book have come from many sources. Some have come from participants in my workshops who started using learning contracts in their practice and sent me copies of contracts negotiated with their learners. Others have come from people who heard that I was preparing a book on contract learning and sent me examples from their practice for me to consider. And others have come from institutions that I heard were using contracts and wrote to requesting examples. The resulting collection is not a product of an extensive survey but of informal networking. It is not intended, therefore, to be an exhaustive collection but only a more or less illustrative one. I hope that it will be helpful in stimulating further experimentation and refinement of the contract learning process.

The book is organized into two parts. Part One, "Understanding Contract Learning," opens with an invitation to readers to have a hands-on experience in constructing a contract for themselves (Chapter One), then explores the theory and practice of contract learning (Chapter Two), and closes with case descriptions of the experience of three institutions in introducing contract learning into their programs (Chapter Three). Part Two, "Developing and Using Learning Contracts in Various Settings," includes examples of contracts and descriptions of how they were developed in independent study (Chapter Four), academic classroom courses (Chapter Five), clinical placements, graduate assistantships, and internships (Chapter Six), continuing professional and management development (Chapter Seven), and total degree programs (Chapter Eight). In the concluding chapter, "Practical Hints on Achieving Success with Contract Learning," I urge readers to examine contracts in various contexts, since contracts developed in one context may suggest ideas that could easily be adapted to others.

I owe a debt of gratitude to the many practitioners who submitted examples of their contracts and gave permission for me to reproduce them, and I wish to express my regrets to the equal number who submitted examples that could not be fitted into the space allocated for this book. I want especially to thank Len and Zeace Nadler, consulting editors for Jossey-Bass, Alan B. Knox of the University of Wisconsin, and Clark Taylor of the University of Massachusetts at Boston for their help in putting this book into final shape.

I hope that this is just the first edition of this book, and I invite practitioners who are using learning contracts—especially in settings not well represented here, such as human resource development in business and industry, noncredit continuing education, and voluntary organizations—to send me examples of actual contracts and brief descriptions of how they were developed for inclusion in a subsequent edition.

Raleigh, North Carolina   Malcolm S. Knowles
September 1986

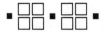

The Author

Malcolm S. Knowles is professor emeritus of adult and community college education at North Carolina State University and previously was professor of education at Boston University, executive director of the Adult Education Association of the U.S.A., and director of adult education at the YMCAs in Boston, Detroit, and Chicago. He received his B.A. degree (1934) from Harvard College and his M.A. degree (1949) and his Ph.D. degree (1960) from the University of Chicago—all in education. He has honorary degrees from Lowell Technical Institute, the National College of Education, and Regis College.

Knowles's main academic and professional interests have been in the theory and practice of adult education. In addition to administering adult education programs and teaching in graduate schools, he has done consulting and conducted workshops for a wide variety of organizations and corporations in North America, Europe, South America, and Australia. His books include *Informal Adult Education* (1950), *Teaching Adults in Informal Courses* (1954), *How to Develop Better Leaders* (with Hulda Knowles, 1955), *Introduction to Group Dynamics* (with Hulda Knowles, 1959; rev. ed., 1972), *Handbook of Adult Education in the U.S.* (editor, 1962), *The Adult Education Movement in the U.S.* (1962; rev. ed., 1977), *Higher Adult Education in the United States* (1969), *The Modern Practice of Adult Education: From Pedagogy to Andragogy* (1970; rev. ed., 1980), *The Adult Learner: A Neglected Species* (1973; rev. ed., 1984), *Self-Directed Learning: A Guide for Learners and Teachers* (1975), and *Andragogy in Action: Applying Principles of Adult Learning* (with others, 1984).

During his retirement, Knowles is serving as a mentor for the Fielding Institute's external degree program in human and organizational development, as national lecturer for the Nova University Center for Higher Education, as adjunct professor of the Union Graduate School, and as a member of the Task Force on Lifelong Education of the UNESCO Institute for Education, for which he has written a chapter, "Creating Lifelong Learning Communities," for its forthcoming book on lifelong education.

Using Learning Contracts

*Practical Approaches to
Individualizing and
Structuring Learning*

ONE

The Contract Learning Process: A Hands-On Experience

■ *David A. Kolb (1981), in his experiential learning theory, proposes that when we undertake to learn something through our own initiative, we start with a concrete experience. Then we make observations about and reflect on that experience and diagnose what new knowledge or skill we need to acquire in order to perform more effectively. Then, with the help of material and human resources, we formulate abstract concepts and generalizations from which new implications for action can be deduced. Finally, we test these concepts and generalizations in new situations.*

Following Kolb's lead, I am opening this inquiry by providing the reader with a concrete experience with the process of contract learning.

The experience I have chosen is the process I used in a seminar, "The Theory and Practice of Adult Education Methodology," with the West Florida Cluster of the Center for Higher Education of Nova University. The seminar met with me as the "national lecturer" all day one Saturday a month for three months. About a month before the first meeting, each learner received a study guide that contained a statement of purpose (in the form of answers to the question "Why should people spend time and energy studying adult education methods?"), assumptions about learners and learning on which the seminar was based, a Competency Diagnostic and Planning Guide, a set of guidelines for constructing a learning contract, the seminar objectives and process design, inquiry units related to the objectives, and source references relevant to each inquiry unit (the sources referred to are listed in the accompanying bibliography).

The study guide instructed the learners to diagnose their learning needs by means of the competency rating scale and to come to the first meeting of the cluster with a draft of a learning contract. The first morning was spent having the learners review one another's contracts in

1

triads, and I reviewed them over lunch. The learners were then organized into "inquiry teams," each team taking responsibility for one or more of the inquiry units. During the remainder of the cluster meeting time, the teams did their research and presented their findings.

This chapter reproduces the study guide, with permission of Nova University, and the contract of one of the learners, a counselor in a community college. Note how the contract makes use of the learner's inquiry team ("consultant group"), colleagues at his community college, the national lecturer, and others for verification of his evidence. Since Nova University uses a pass/fail grading system, no grade was specified in the contract.

After the presentation of the contract I shall make some observations and do some reflecting. Some generalizations about contract learning will be provided in Chapter Two.

■ SELECTION 1
Study Guide: The Theory and Practice of Adult Education Methodology

Introduction

Purpose

Why should people who have been exposed to teaching methods through years of being taught (and, perhaps, also through years of teaching) now spend time and energy studying adult education methods? For several reasons.

For one thing, the methods of adult education have been becoming more and more different from the methods of traditional schooling as we have gained increased knowledge about the unique characteristics of adults as learners. Teachers who only know how to teach adults as they themselves were taught in school tend to be ineffective in most situations.

For another thing, the technology of adult education has been in a state of ferment. During the past three decades we have experienced wave after wave of new inventions that tend to take on the character of fads, in the sense that some people get so enamored of one technique that they use it in every situation whether it is appropriate or not. The ability to incorporate new techniques into a growing repertoire of techniques and then choose the technique that is most effective for accomplishing a particular educational objective is a competence that separates the professionals from the amateurs in adult education. This ability grows out of their having an understanding of a good theory of adult education methodology.

Finally, we now have a coherent, comprehensive, and integrated theory of adult learning that requires a redefinition of the role of teacher. In traditional education the teacher has been defined as one who decides what should be learned, how it should be learned, when it should be learned, and whether it has been learned—the role of content planner, controller, transmitter, and evaluator. In the modern adult education (andragogical) model, the teacher is defined as one who designs a process and manages the procedures for helping learners to identify learning needs and then to acquire the content necessary to meet those needs—the role of facilitator and resource person for self-directed learners. This new role requires a very different set of skills and attitudes from those of the traditional teacher.

The purpose of this seminar, therefore, is to help participants accomplish three broad objectives:

1. The development of increased skill in designing learning experiences that are geared to the unique characteristics of adults as learners.
2. The development of clearer rationales and deeper insights regarding the selection of particular methods, techniques, and materials for achieving particular learning objectives.
3. The broadening of the participants' repertoire of skills in using a variety of methods and techniques.

Definitions

The technology of adult education is still in such an early formative stage that a standardized lexicon of its terminology has not yet emerged. As a result, writers in the field—and practitioners as well—use a variety of labels to describe the same phenomena. A start has been made to bring order out of this chaos by Dr. Coolie Verner of the University of British Columbia. Verner distinguishes three elements in the notion of processes for adult education, each of which describes a separate function:

> The first element is the method: the organization of the prospective participants for purposes of education. The second element involves *techniques*: the variety of ways in which the learning task is managed so as to facilitate learning. The third and final element involves *devices*: all those particular things or conditions which are utilized to augment the techniques and make learning more certain [Verner, 1962, pp. 9-10].

Verner elaborates on his concept of method as follows:

> The method of education identifies the ways in which people are organized in order to conduct an educational activity. A method establishes a relationship between the learner and the institution or agency through which the educational task is accomplished. Formal educational institutions establish such a relationship for learning by having the participants come to the institution and organizing them into groups according to age, ability, subject matter, or some other criterion. These groups are referred to as classes. Since pre-adult education is almost exclusively institutionalized through the school, the principal method employed is the class. Adult education, on the other hand, is not exclusively institutionalized; therefore, it employs the class method as only one in a variety of methods.
>
> Because the method describes a way of organizing participants, the methods of adult education tend to fall into a classification scheme that is predetermined by the ways in which people are naturally organized in the society. People may be found as isolated individuals, as small or large aggregations, or collected into communities. Thus, the methods of adult education can be classified as individual, group, or community methods [Verner and Booth, 1964, pp. 68-69].

In this study guide *format* is used with precisely the same meaning that Verner gives to *method*. *Format* is preferred because it seems to convey more of a sense of a structural element and because it is more clearly separated from *technique* than *method*.

Assumptions About Learners and Learning

This study guide makes certain assumptions about adults as learners and the learning process that have some implications for what you do and how you will use the national lecturer and resource materials.

First, about you as an adult learner, it assumes:

1. That you have the self-concept of being an adult, and therefore you have the desire and capability of taking responsibility for planning and managing your own learning—with help, of course, from peers, cluster coordinators, national lecturers, and other helpers. It further assumes that what you learn through your own initiative you will learn more effectively than what you learn through imposition by others.

2. That you bring with you into this activity a rich background of experience that is a valuable resource both for your own learning and for the learning of others in the cluster. It further assumes that your experience is different from the experiences of the other members of the cluster and that therefore your combined experiences represent a rich pool of resources for one another's learning.

3. That you are readiest to learn those things that you perceive will contribute to your performing more effectively in your life tasks and to your achieving a higher level of your potential. It further assumes that the study guide itself, the cluster coordinator, and the national lecturers have an obligation to help you see how the content of the seminar will help you perform more effectively.

4. That you and every other member of the cluster group are unique, with your own styles and paces of learning, outside commitments and pressures, goals, and internal motivations, and that therefore your learning plans and strategies must be highly individualized.

Next, about learning, the study guide assumes that learning is an internal process with the locus of control of that process residing in the learner but that this process can be facilitated by outside helpers. It further assumes that there are certain conditions that are more conducive to learning than others and that these superior conditions are produced by practices in the learning-teaching transaction that adhere to certain superior principles of teaching. These conditions and principles are described below, the term *facilitators* being used with the meaning of study guide, cluster coordinator, national lecturer, and other members of the cluster.

Conditions of Learning	*Principles of Teaching*
The learners feel the need to learn.	1. The facilitators expose the learners to new possibilities for self-fulfillment. 2. The facilitators help the learners clarify their own aspirations for improved performance. 3. The facilitators help the learners diagnose the gaps between their aspirations and their present level of performance.
The learning environment is characterized by physical comfort, mutual respect and trust, mutual helpfulness, freedom of expression, and acceptance of differences.	4. The facilitators provide physical conditions that are comfortable (as to seating, temperature, ventilation, lighting, decoration) and conducive to interaction (circle or small groups at tables). 5. The facilitators accept the learners as persons of worth and respect their feelings and ideas. 6. The facilitators build relationships of mutual trust and helpfulness with and among the learners by encouraging cooperative activities and refraining from inducing competitiveness and judgmentalness. 7. The facilitators expose their own feelings and contribute their resources in the spirit of mutual inquiry.
The learners perceive the goals of the learning experience to be their goals.	8. The facilitators involve the students in a mutual process of formulating learning objectives in which the needs of the learners, of the facilitators, of the institution, of the subject matter, and of society are taken into account.

The learners accept a
share of the responsibility
for planning and operat-
ing the learning
experience.

The learners participate
actively in the learning
process.

The learning process is related to and makes use of
the experience of the
learners.

9. The facilitators shape their
   thinking about the options available in designing learning experiences and the selection of methods and materials and involve the
   learners in deciding among these
   options jointly.
10. The facilitators help the students
    organize themselves (project
    teams, field projects, and so on)
    to share responsibility in the pro-
    cess of mutual inquiry.
11. The facilitators help the learners
    exploit their own experiences as
    resources for learning through
    such techniques as group discus-
    sion, case method, and projects.
12. The facilitators gear the presen-
    tation of their own resources to
    the levels of experience of the
    learners.
13. The facilitators help the learners
    to apply new learnings to their
    personal experiences and thus to
    make the learnings more relevant
    and integrated.

The learners have a sense
of progress toward their
goals.

14. The facilitators involve the
    learners in developing mutually
    acceptable progress toward the
    learning objectives.
15. The facilitators help the learners
    develop and apply procedures for
    self-evaluation according to these
    criteria.

In accordance with these assumptions, this study guide
employs a competency-based, self-directed learning approach.

Preparatory Activities

The value of the first meeting with the national lecturer and the other cluster members will be greatly enhanced if you accomplish the following tasks before the first meeting:

1. Read Part I (pp. 7–28) of *Self-Directed Learning* by Malcolm Knowles (if you have not done so previously) so as to have at least a beginning grasp of what is involved in your taking a high degree of responsibility for your own learning.

2. Scan the other two basic references (Knowles, *The Modern Practice of Adult Education,* especially chap. 11, and Hospital Continuing Education Project, *Training and Continuing Education,* especially chaps. 7–11) so as to get a broad-stroke overview of the territory covered in this seminar.

3. Turn to Appendix A of this study guide, the "Competency Diagnostic and Planning Guide," and rate each competency in terms of (1) its importance to your career or self-actualization, (2) the level to which you have presently developed it, and (3) its level of priority for further development in this seminar. Don't be afraid to follow your intuition at this point in making these ratings, but later you may want to take the diagnostic guide to several people who know you and ask them to react to your self-rating. You may want to write in additional competencies of your own. Notice that the competencies are coded to coincide with the items in the inquiry units.

4. Now prepare a first draft of a learning contract. As a first step, turn to Appendix B, "Some Guidelines for the Use of Learning Contracts in Learning," and read it carefully, paying special attention to Steps 4 and 5, which is where people doing this for the first time typically have the most difficulty. Then turn to Appendix C, "Sample Learning Contract," and see what a completed contract looks like. Now go back to your diagnostic guide and translate each competency that is rated at a medium to high level of priority into a learning objective. Insert these objectives into column one of Appendix D, "Learning Contract," and fill in the remaining columns of the contract form in accordance with the guidelines. Don't worry about feeling awkward or inadequate at this point; you will get further help at

the first meeting and will be able to revise your contract at any point up to the end of the seminar. *Please bring two copies of the completed contract with you to the first meeting.*

5. Finally, complete as much as you can of that part of your contract having to do with Unit 1 of the study guide, "Designing Learning Experiences." This unit will be the focus of the discussion at the first meeting.

Process Design for the Seminar

First Session

9:00–9:45 A.M.: Climate setting
- The national lecturer will explain the importance of creating a climate that is conducive to learning—a climate that is characterized by mutual respect, warmth and supportiveness of relationships, active participation, collaboration rather than competition, and acknowledgment of the concerns and interests of the learners—as a prerequisite for the effective learning to take place.
- Participants form themselves into groups of from three to five persons each (preferably with people they don't already know well) and share these things within each group (with one member of each group volunteering to give a summary at the end of the period):
  1. What they are (in Martin Buber's terms, their "its")—their present work roles and previous experience.
  2. Who they are (Buber's "I-Thou")—one thing about themselves that will enable others to see them as unique human beings, different from everyone else in the room.
  3. Any special resources which are relevant to this seminar (previous experience or study) that would be useful for others to know about.
  4. Any concerns, problems, curiosities, or issues that they are hoping to have this seminar deal with.

- The national lecturer will retrieve this information by asking the group reporters to give their summaries.

9:45–10:15 A.M.: Self-introduction by the national lecturer

- The national lecturer will share the above information about himself or herself, plus anything else he or she wants to say about his or her role.

10:15–10:30 A.M.: Break

10:30–11:00 A.M.: Review of self-diagnosed learning needs

- Participants form into "consultation teams" (groups of two or three) and help one another check out how realistic their ratings on their "Competency Diagnostic and Planning Guide" are.

11:00 A.M.–noon: Review of learning contracts

- Consultation teams help one another review their contracts (see Step 6 of "Some Guidelines for the Use of Learning Contracts in Learning").

Noon–1:00 P.M.: Lunch

1:00–1:30 P.M.: Census of content issues for Unit 1

- New groups of four or five persons form to agree on questions or issues regarding the content of Inquiry Unit 1 ("Designing Learning Experiences") they would like to discuss with the national lecturer.

1:30–3:00 P.M.: Discussion

- The groups pose their questions and issues and the national lecturer responds.

3:00–3:15 P.M.: Break

3:15–4:00 P.M.: Continuation of discussion

4:00–4:15 P.M.: Organization of inquiry teams for Inquiry Unit 2

- Participants volunteer to take responsibility for in-depth investigation of one or more of the questions in Unit 2 and to share findings at the second session (teams of from one to three).

4:15–4:30 P.M.: Formative evaluation

- Participants share observations about the procedures used in this session and make suggestions for the second session.

4:30 P.M.: National lecturer collects one copy of the learning contracts (unless some participants wish to make revisions and mail contract).

Between the First and Second Sessions

1. Complete the learning strategies, collection of evidence, and verification of evidence for Inquiry Unit 1 as provided for in the learning contract.
2. Carry out the contract's specifications for Unit 2, which will be the subject for discussion at the second session. (Learning contracts will have been returned, with comments, by national lecturer by mail.)

Second Session

9:00–10:15 A.M.: Sharing of findings of inquiry teams
  ▪ Inquiry teams report their findings regarding the questions in Unit 2, "Selecting Methods, Techniques, and Materials."
10:15–10:30 A.M.: Break
10:30–11:30 A.M.: Continuation of reports of inquiry teams
11:30 A.M.–noon: Census of content issues for Unit 2
  ▪ Groups of four or five persons agree on questions or issues regarding the content of Inquiry Unit 2 they would like to discuss with the national lecturer.
Noon–1:00 P.M.: Lunch
1:00–3:00 P.M.: Discussion
  ▪ The groups pose their questions and issues and the national lecturer responds.
3:00–3:15 P.M.: Break
3:15–4:00 P.M.: Continuation of discussion
4:00–4:15 P.M.: Organization of inquiry teams for Inquiry Unit 3
4:15–4:30 P.M.: Formative evaluation

Between the Second and Third Sessions

1. Execute learning contract for Unit 3.

2. Complete the portfolio of evidence as specified in contract and bring to third session.

Third Session

> 9:00–10:15 A.M.: Sharing of findings of inquiry teams regarding questions in Inquiry Unit 3, "Skill in Using a Broad Spectrum of Techniques"
>
> 10:15–10:30 A.M.: Break
>
> 10:30–11:30 A.M.: Continuation of reports of inquiry teams
>
> 11:30 A.M.–noon: Census of content issues for Unit 3
>
> - Groups of four or five agree on questions or issues regarding the content of Unit 3 that they would like to discuss with the national lecturer.
>
> Noon–1:00 P.M.: Lunch
>
> 1:00–3:00 P.M.: Discussion
>
> - The groups pose their questions and issues and the national lecturer responds.
>
> 3:00–3:15 P.M.: Break
>
> 3:15–4:15 P.M.: Review of portfolios of evidence
>
> - Consultation teams of three or four review one another's portfolios of evidence and make suggestions for improvement.
>
> 4:15–4:45 P.M.: Summative evaluation
>
> - Participants share their observations about the seminar as a whole and make suggestions for improvement.
>
> 4:45 P.M.: Portfolios of evidence are collected by the national lecturer, who will mail them back to participants.

Inquiry Units

Unit 1: Designing Learning Experiences

> 1.1 What are the unique characteristics of adult learners to which learning experiences must be geared?
> *Sources*: Knowles, *The Modern Practice of Adult Education*, chap. 4; Knowles, *The Adult Learner: A Neglected Species*, chap. 3; Kidd, *How Adults Learn*, chap. 2; Knox,

Adult Development and Learning, chap. 7.

1.2 What is the process of designing learning experiences? (How are process designs different from content plans?)
Sources: Knowles, *The Modern Practice of Adult Education*, chaps. 8, 11; Knowles, *The Adult Learner*, pp. 108–129; Knowles, *Self-Directed Learning*, pp. 31–38; Houle, *The Design of Education*, chaps. 2, 5; Kidd, *How Adults Learn*, chap. 10. For designing workshops, see Davis and McCallon, *Planning, Conducting, Evaluating Workshops*, and Nadler and Nadler, *The Conference Book*.

1.3 What is the role of the teacher in designing and managing learning experiences?
Sources: Knowles, *The Modern Practice of Adult Education*, chaps. 2, 3, 11; Knowles, *Self-Directed Learning*, pp. 44–58; Kidd, *How Adults Learn*, chap. 11.

1.4 How can adults be helped to make the transition from teacher-directed learners to self-directed learners?
Sources: Knowles, *Self-Directed Learning*, pp. 39–43; Tough, *The Adult's Learning Projects*, chaps. 9, 10.

Unit 2: Selecting Methods, Techniques, and Materials

2.1 What is the broad range of methods, techniques, and materials available to help adults learn?
Sources: Knowles, *The Modern Practice of Adult Education*, chap. 11; Hospital Continuing Education Project, *Training and Continuing Education*, chaps. 7–11. See also works in the bibliography by Aker; Benne, Bradford, and Lippitt; Bergevin and McKinley; Carlson; Otto; Pfeiffer and Jones; Pigors; Russell; Schid and Boocock; and Thayer.

2.2 What methods and techniques are most effective for achieving particular learning objectives?
Sources: Knowles, *The Modern Practice of Adult Education*, exhibit 33; Hospital Continuing Education Project, *Training and Continuing Education*, chap. 10.

Unit 3: Skill in Using a Broad Spectrum of Techniques

For this unit each participant will select those techniques in the list below requiring strengthening and, alone or with one or two other participants with the same needs, will practice using the techniques until he or she has developed confidence in using them. Time may be allocated in the third session for participants to demonstrate techniques and get feedback on their performances. The broad spectrum of techniques includes at least the following:

3.1 *Climate-setting techniques*
  ■ Presenting oneself as an authentic human being
  ■ Various ways of getting learners to get acquainted with one another
  ■ Getting the learners to identify their resources from previous training or experience
  ■ Skill-practice exercises in self-directed learning

3.2 *Diagnostic techniques*
  ■ Constructing a competency model
  ■ Constructing and conducting performance-assessment tools and procedures
  ■ Conducting diagnostic interviews
  ■ Administering diagnostic tests (standardized)

3.3 *Presentation techniques*
  ■ Lecture
  ■ Television, videotape
  ■ Debate
  ■ Dialogue
  ■ Group interview
  ■ Symposium
  ■ Panel discussion
  ■ Demonstration
  ■ Colloquy
  ■ Audiocassette
  ■ Programmed instruction
  ■ Multimedia packages
  ■ Motion picture
  ■ Slides
  ■ Dramatization
  ■ Recordings
  ■ Exhibits
  ■ Trips
  ■ Readings

3.4 *Audience participation techniques*
  ■ Question-and-answer period
  ■ Forum
  ■ Listening teams
  ■ Reaction panel
  ■ Buzz groups
  ■ Audience role playing
  ■ Expanding panel

3.5 *Discussion and counseling techniques*
- Guided discussion
- Book-based discussion
- Socratic discussion
- Problem-solving discussion
- Case discussion
- Group-centered discussion
- Coaching and counseling

3.6 *Simulation techniques*
- Role playing
- Critical-incident process
- Case method
- Simulation exercises
- Games
- Action maze
- Participative cases

3.7 *Group process techniques*
- T-groups (sensitivity training)
- Transactional Analysis
- Gestalt groups

3.8 *Audiovisual and other resource materials*
- Audiovisual materials
- Study guides, workbooks, and so forth
- Programmed learning and computer-managed instructional materials

3.9 *Evaluation techniques*
- Questionnaires and rating scales
- See "Diagnostic techniques"

Resources

A number of sources of information have been cited under each of the questions in the inquiry units in the previous section. This has been done not because all of the sources are necessary to obtain satisfactory answers to the questions but because not all of the references will be available in all locations. You are urged, however, to scour other depositories than your own institution's library to try to locate references that are important to your inquiry, including public libraries (which may be able to obtain works they don't themselves have, through interlibrary loan); the libraries of nearby community colleges, colleges, and universities; the professional libraries of adult educators in your community (industrial trainers, government staff development officers,

Cooperative Extension Service agents, trainers in voluntary organizations, religious adult educators); and public school libraries.

Perhaps the single richest source of information about methods and techniques that are geared specifically to adults as learners is the publications of University Associates, Box 80637, San Diego, California 92138. Its series *Handbooks of Structured Experiences for Human Relations Training* is especially useful.

A Master Bibliography, which lists many more references than those cited in this study guide, is available for $5.00 from the Center for Higher Education at Nova.

Finally, the Office of Information Services at Nova has computer access to the Educational Resources Information Center (ERIC) and more than 100 other data bases and will do computer searches of these data bases for you. A computer search results in a printout of citations of documents that meet your specifications. It is available for a small fee that usually can be paid for with cluster operating funds. In addition, the Office of Information Services has a large collection of documents on microfiche that can be obtained free of charge.

Bibliography

Basic References (which each participant should own)

Hospital Continuing Education Project. *Training and Continuing Education: A Handbook for Health Care Institutions.* Chicago: Hospital Research and Educational Trust (840 North Lake Shore Drive, Chicago, Ill. 60611), 1970.

Knowles, M. S. *Self-Directed Learning: A Guide for Learners and Teachers.* New York: Cambridge Book Company, 1975.

Knowles, M. S. *The Modern Practice of Adult Education: From Pedagogy to Andragogy.* (2nd ed.) New York: Cambridge Book Company, 1980.

Supplemental References

Aker, G. F. *Adult Education Procedures, Methods, and Techniques: A Classified and Annotated Bibliography, 1953–1963.* Syracuse, N.Y.: Library of Continuing Education, Syracuse University Press, 1965.

Benne, K., Bradford, L., and Lippitt, R. *The Laboratory Method of Changing and Learning: Theory and Application.* Palo Alto, Calif.: Science and Behavior Books, 1975.

Bergevin, P., and McKinley, J. *Participation Training for Adult Education.* St. Louis, Mo.: Bethany Press, 1965.

Berte, N. R. *Individualizing Education by Learning Contracts.* New Directions for Higher Education, no. 10. San Francisco: Jossey-Bass, 1975.

Carlson, E. *Learning Through Games.* New York: Public Affairs Press, 1970.

Craig, R. L. (ed.). *Training and Development Handbook.* (2nd ed.) New York: McGraw-Hill, 1976.

Davis, L. N., and McCallon, E. *Planning, Conducting, Evaluating Workshops.* Austin, Texas: Learning Concepts, 1974.

Dickinson, G. *Teaching Adults: A Handbook for Instructors.* Toronto: New Press, 1973.

Eble, K. E. *The Craft of Teaching: A Guide to Mastering the Professor's Art.* San Francisco: Jossey-Bass, 1976.

Ingalls, J. D., and Arceri, J. M. *A Trainers' Guide to Andragogy.* SRS 72-05301. U.S. Department of Health, Education and Welfare. Washington, D.C.: U.S. Government Printing Office, 1972.

James, M., and Jongeward, D. *Born to Win: Transactional Analysis with Gestalt Experiments.* Reading, Mass.: Addison-Wesley, 1971.

Jongeward, D., and James, M. *Winning with People: Group Exercises in Transactional Analysis.* Reading, Mass.: Addison-Wesley, 1973.

Kidd, J. R. *How Adults Learn.* New York: Cambridge University Press, 1973.

Klevins, C. (ed.). *Materials and Methods in Adult Education.* Los Angeles: Klevins, 1976.

Knowles, M. S. *The Adult Learner: A Neglected Species.* (3rd ed.) Houston: Gulf, 1984.

Knox, A. B. *Adult Development and Learning: A Handbook on Individual Growth and Competence in the Adult Years.* San Francisco: Jossey-Bass, 1977.

Leypoldt, M. M. *Forty Ways to Teach in Groups.* Valley Forge, Pa.: Judson Press, 1967.

Loughary, J. W., and Hopson, B. *Producing Workshops, Seminars, Short Courses: A Trainer's Handbook.* Chicago: Association Press/Follett, 1979.

McKinley, J. *Creative Methods for Adult Classes.* St. Louis, Mo.: Bethany Press, 1960.

McLagan, P. A. *Helping Others Learn: Designing Programs for Adults.* Reading, Mass.: Addison-Wesley, 1978.

Miller, H. L. *Teaching and Learning in Adult Education.* New York: Macmillan, 1964.

Nadler, L., and Nadler, Z. *The Conference Book.* Houston: Gulf, 1977.

Otto, H. A. *Group Methods to Actualize Human Potential.* La Jolla, Calif.: National Center for the Exploration of Human Potential, 1970.

Pfeiffer, W. J., and Jones, J. E. *A Handbook of Structured Experiences for Human Relations Training.* Issued almost annually since 1969. San Diego, Calif.: University Associates.

Pigors, P. *Case Method in Human Relations: The Incident Process.* New York: McGraw-Hill, 1961.

Russell, J. D. *Modular Instruction.* Minneapolis: Burgess Press, 1974.

Schid, E. O., and Boocock, S. *Simulation Games in Learning.* Beverly Hills: Sage, 1970.

Simon, S. B., Howe, L. W., and Kirschenbaum, H. *Values Clarification.* New York: Hart, 1972.

Smith, M. *A Practical Guide to Value Clarification.* San Diego, Calif.: University Associates, 1977.

Thayer, L. (ed.). *Affective Education: Strategies for Experiential Learning.* San Diego, Calif.: University Associates, 1976.

Tough, A. *The Adult's Learning Projects.* Toronto: Ontario Institute for Studies in Education, 1979.

Verner, C. *A Conceptual Scheme for the Identification and Classification of Processes.* Washington, D.C.: Adult Education Association of the U.S.A., 1962.

Verner, C., and Booth, A. *Adult Education.* Washington, D.C.: Center for Applied Research in Education, 1964.

APPENDIX A
Competency Diagnostic and Planning Guide
The Theory and Practice of Adult Education Methodology

	Importance to My Career or Self-Actualization				Level of Present Development				Level of Priority			
	None	Low	Med.	High	None	Low	Med.	High	None	Low	Med.	High
Unit 1: Designing Learning Experiences												
1.1: *Characteristics of Adult Learners*												
1.1.1: Ability to describe and apply modern concepts and research findings regarding the needs, interests, motivations, capacities, and developmental characteristics of adults as learners.												
1.1.2: Ability to describe the differences between youth and adults as learners and the implications of these differences for teaching and learning.												
1.1.3: Ability to assess the effects on learning of forces impinging on learners from the larger environment (groups, organizations, communities).												
1.2: *The Process of Designing Learning Experiences*												
1.2.1: Ability to describe the difference between a content plan and a process design.												
1.2.2: Ability to design learning experiences for accomplishing a variety of purposes and that take into account individual differences												

1.3: *Role of the Teacher*

1.3.1: Ability to conceptualize and explain the role of the teacher as a facilitator and resource to self-directed learners.

1.3.2: Ability to engineer a physical and psychological climate of mutual respect, trust, collaboration, openness, supportiveness, and safety.

1.3.3: Ability to establish a warm, empathic, facilitative relationship with learners of all sorts.

1.3.4: Ability to engage learners responsibly in self-diagnosis of needs for learning.

1.3.5: Ability to engage learners in formulating goals, objectives, and directions of growth in terms that are meaningful to them.

1.3.6: Ability to involve learners in the planning, conducting, and evaluating of learning activities appropriately.

1.4: *Helping Learners Become Self-Directing*

1.4.1: Ability to explain the conceptual differences between didactic instruction and self-directed learning.

1.4.2: Ability to design and conduct one-hour, three-hour, one-day, and three-day learning experiences to develop the skills of self-directed learning.

1.4.3: Ability to model the role of a self-directed learner in your own behavior.

APPENDIX A, Cont'd.

	Importance to My Career or Self-Actualization				Level of Present Development				Level of Priority			
	None	Low	Med.	High	None	Low	Med.	High	None	Low	Med.	High

Unit 2: Selecting Methods, Techniques, and Materials

2.1: *The Broad Range of Methods, Techniques, and Materials*

2.1.1: Ability to describe the range of methods or formats for organizing learning experiences.

2.1.2: Ability to describe the range of techniques available for facilitating learning.

2.1.3: Ability to describe the range of materials available as resources for learning.

2.2: *Methods and Techniques for Achieving Particular Learning Objectives*

2.2.1: Ability to describe the various theories of learning and their implications for the selection of methods, techniques, and materials.

2.2.2: Ability to provide a rationale for selecting a particular method, technique, or material for achieving a particular educational objective.

2.2.3: Ability to evaluate various methods, techniques, and materials as to their effectiveness in achieving particular educational outcomes.

Unit 3: **Skill in Using a Broad Spectrum of Techniques**

3.1: *Climate-Setting Techniques*

3.1.1: Ability to present oneself as an authentic human being, not just one performing the role of teacher.

3.1.2: Ability to use several different techniques for helping learners become acquainted with one another.

3.1.3: Ability to use several techniques for helping learners identify their resources (from previous training or experience).

3.1.4: Ability to conduct several skill-practice exercises in self-directed learning.

3.2: *Diagnostic Techniques*

3.2.1: Ability to develop and manage procedures for the construction of models of competency.

3.2.2: Ability to develop and manage procedures for constructing performance assessment tools and procedures.

3.2.3: Ability to conduct diagnostic interviews.

3.2.4: Ability to administer achievement tests, aptitude tests, and other standardized diagnostic tests.

3.3: *Presentation Techniques*

3.3.1: Ability to present information, provide inspiration, and stimulate inquiry through lectures effectively.

3.3.2: Ability to use television and videotape programs appropriately.

APPENDIX A, Cont'd.

	Importance to My Career or Self-Actualization				Level of Present Development				Level of Priority			
	None	Low	Med.	High	None	Low	Med.	High	None	Low	Med.	High
3.3.3: Ability to use a variety of platform techniques, including debate, dialogue, group interview, symposium, panel discussion, demonstration, colloquy.												
3.3.4: Ability to use audiocassette programs appropriately.												
3.3.5: Ability to use programmed instruction appropriately.												
3.3.6: Ability to select or construct multimedia package programs appropriately.												
3.3.7: Ability to use motion pictures, filmstrips, and slides appropriately.												
3.3.8: Ability to use dramatization techniques appropriately.												
3.3.9: Ability to use recordings appropriately.												
3.3.10: Ability to use exhibits as a resource for learning.												
3.3.11: Ability to use trips as a resource for learning.												
3.4: *Audience Participation Techniques (Large Meetings)*												
3.4.1: Ability to use question-and-answer period effectively.												

3.4.2:	Ability to use the forum technique.							
3.4.3:	Ability to use listening teams.							
3.4.4:	Ability to use reaction panels.							
3.4.5:	Ability to use buzz groups.							
3.4.6:	Ability to use audience role playing.							
3.5:	*Discussion and Counseling Techniques*							
3.5.1:	Ability to lead guided discussion.							
3.5.2:	Ability to use book-based discussion.							
3.5.3:	Ability to lead Socratic discussion.							
3.5.4:	Ability to lead problem-solving discussion.							
3.5.5:	Ability to lead case discussion.							
3.5.6:	Ability to lead group-centered discussion.							
3.5.7:	Ability to use coaching and counseling techniques.							
3.6:	*Simulation Techniques*							
3.6.1:	Ability to use role playing.							
3.6.2:	Ability to use the critical-incident process.							
3.6.3:	Ability to use the case method.							
3.6.4:	Ability to use simulation and skill-practice exercises.							
3.6.5:	Ability to use gaming techniques.							
3.6.6:	Ability to use the action maze.							
3.6.7:	Ability to use participative cases.							
3.7:	*Group Process Techniques*							
3.7.1:	Ability to use human relations laboratory and sensitivity training techniques.							

APPENDIX A, Cont'd.

	Importance to My Career or Self-Actualization				Level of Present Development				Level of Priority			
	None	Low	Med.	High	None	Low	Med.	High	None	Low	Med.	High
3.7.2: Ability to use Transactional Analysis.												
3.7.3: Ability to use Gestalt techniques.												
3.8: *Audiovisual and Other Resource Materials*												
3.8.1: Ability to construct and use a wide variety of audiovisual materials.												
3.8.2: Ability to construct study guides, work-books, and other teacher-made materials.												
3.8.3: Ability to develop programmed learning and computer-managed instructional materials.												
3.9: *Evaluation Techniques*												
3.9.1: Ability to evaluate learning procedures and outcomes and to select or construct appropriate instruments for this purpose.												
3.9.2: Ability to assess performance before and after a learning experience to measure effects.												

APPENDIX B
Some Guidelines for the Use of Learning Contracts in Learning

Why Use Learning Contracts?

One of the most significant findings from research about adult learning (for example, Allen Tough's *The Adult's Learning Projects*, Ontario Institute for Studies in Education, Toronto, 1979) is that when adults go about learning something naturally (as contrasted with being taught something), they are highly self-directing. Evidence is beginning to accumulate, too, that what adults learn on their own initiative they learn more deeply and permanently than what they learn by being taught.

Those kinds of learning that are engaged in for purely personal development can perhaps be planned and carried out completely by an individual on his or her own terms and with only a loose structure. But those kinds of learning that have as their purpose improving one's competence to perform in a job or in a profession must take into account the needs and expectations of organizations, professions, and society. Learning contracts provide a means for negotiating a reconciliation between these external needs and expectations and the learner's internal needs and interests.

Furthermore, in traditional education the learning activity is structured by the teacher and the institution. The learners are told what objectives they are to work toward, what resources they are to use and how (and when) to use them, and how their accomplishment of the objectives will be evaluated. This imposed structure conflicts with the adult's deep psychological need to be self-directing and may induce resistance, apathy, or withdrawal. Learning contracts provide a vehicle for making the planning of learning experiences a mutual undertaking between a learner and his or her helper, mentor, teacher, and, often, peers. By participating in the process of diagnosing needs, formulating objectives, identifying resources, choosing strategies, and evaluating accomplishments, the learner develops a sense of ownership of (and commitment to) the plan.

Finally, in field-based learning particularly, there is a strong possibility that what is to be learned from the experience will be less clear to both the learner and the field supervisor than what work is to be done. There is a long tradition of field-experience learners being exploited for the performance of menial tasks. The learning contract is a means for making the *learning objectives* of the field experience clear and explicit for both the learner and the field supervisor.

How Do You Develop a Learning Contract?

Step 1: Diagnose your learning needs. A learning need is the gap between where you are now and where you want to be in regard to a particular set of competencies.

You may already be aware of certain learning needs as a result of a personnel appraisal process or the long accumulation of evidence for yourself of the gaps between where you are now and where you would like to be.

If not (or even so), it might be worth your while to go through this process: First, construct a model of the competencies required to perform excellently the role (for example, parent, teacher, civic leader, manager, consumer, professional worker) you are concerned about. There may be a competency model already in existence that you can use as a thought-starter and checklist; many professions are developing such models. If not, you can build your own, with help from friends, colleagues, supervisors, and expert resource people. A competency can be thought of as the ability to do something at some level of proficiency and is usually composed of some combination of knowledge, understanding, skill, attitude, and values. For example, "ability to ride a bicycle from my home to the store" is a competency that involves some knowledge of how a bicycle operates and the route to the store; an understanding of some of the dangers inherent in riding a bicycle; skill in mounting, pedaling, steering, and stopping a bicycle; an attitude of desire to ride a bicycle; and a valuing of the exercise it will yield. "Ability to ride a bicycle in a cross-country race" would be a higher-level competency that would require greater knowledge, understanding, skill, and so on. It is useful to produce a competency model even if it is crude and subjective because of the clearer sense of direction it will give you.

Having constructed a competency model, your next task is to assess the gap between where you are now and where the model says you should be in regard to each competency. You can do this alone or with the help of people who have been observing your performance. The chances are that you will find that you have already developed some competencies to a level of excellence, so that you can concentrate on those you haven't.

Step 2: Specify your learning objectives. You are now ready to start filling out the first column of the learning contract, "Learning Objectives." Each of the learning needs diagnosed in Step 1 should be translated into a learning objective. Be sure that your objectives describe what you will *learn*, not what you will *do* to learn them. State them in terms that are most meaningful to you—content acquisition, terminal behaviors, or directions of growth.

Step 3: Specify learning resources and strategies. When you have finished listing your objectives, move over to the second column of the contract, "Learning Resources and Strategies," and describe how you propose to go about accomplishing each objective. Identify the resources (material and human) you plan to use in your field experience and the strategies (techniques, tools) you will employ in making use of them. Here is an example:

Learning Objective	*Learning Resources and Strategies*
Improve my ability to organize my work efficiently so that I can accomplish 20 percent more work in a day.	1. Find books and articles in library on how to organize your work and manage time and read them.
	2. Interview three executives on how they organize their work, then observe them for one day each, noting techniques they use.
	3. Select the best techniques

from each, plan a day's
work, and have a colleague
observe me for a day, giving
me feedback.

Step 4: Specify evidence of accomplishment. After completing the second column, move over to the fourth column, "Evidence," and describe what evidence you will collect to indicate the
degree to which you have achieved each objective. Perhaps the
following examples of evidence for different types of objectives
will stimulate your thinking about what evidence you might
accumulate:

Type of Objective	*Examples of Evidence*
Knowledge	Reports of knowledge acquired, as in essays, examinations, oral presentations; annotated bibliographies.
Understanding	Examples of utilization of knowledge in solving problems, as in action projects, research projects with conclusions and recommendations, plans for curriculum change, and so on.
Skills	Performance exercises, videotaped performances, and so on, with ratings by observers.
Attitudes	Attitudinal rating scales; performance in real situations, role playing, simulation games, critical-incident cases, and so on, with feedback from participants and/or observers.
Values	Value rating scales; performance in value clarification groups, critical-incident cases, simulation exercises, and so on, with feedback from participants and/or observers.

Step 5: Specify how the evidence will be validated. After you have specified what evidence you will gather for each objective in column four, move over to column five, "Verification." For each objective, first specify what criteria will vary according to the type of objective. For example, appropriate criteria for knowledge objectives might include comprehensiveness, depth, precision, clarity, authentication and usefulness, and scholarliness. For skill objectives more appropriate criteria may be poise, speed, flexibility, gracefulness, precision, and imaginativeness. After you have specified the criteria, indicate the means you propose to use to have the evidence judged according to these criteria. For example, if you produce a paper or report, whom will you have read it and what are those persons' qualifications? Will they express their judgments by rating scales, descriptive reports, evaluative reports, or how? One of the actions that help to differentiate "distinguished" from "adequate" performance in self-directed learning is the wisdom with which a learner selects his or her validators.

Step 6: Review your contract with consultants. After you have completed the first draft of your contract, you will find it useful to review it with two or three friends, supervisors, or other expert resource people to get their reactions and suggestions. Here are some questions you might have them ask about the contract to get optimal benefit from their help:

- Are the learning objectives clear, understandable, and realistic; and do they describe what you propose to learn?
- Can they think of other objectives you might consider?
- Do the learning strategies and resources seem reasonable, appropriate, and efficient?
- Can they think of other resources and strategies you might consider?
- Does the evidence seem relevant to the various objectives, and would it convince them?
- Can they suggest other evidence you might consider?
- Are the criteria and means for validating the evidence clear, relevant, and convincing?
- Can they think of other ways to validate the evidence that you might consider?

■   Can they think of other ways to validate the evidence that you
    might consider?

Step 7: Carry out the contract. You now simply do what the
contract calls for. But keep in mind that as you work on it you
may find that your notions about what you want to learn and how
you want to learn it may change. So don't hesitate to revise your
contract as you go along.

Step 8: Evaluation of your learning. When you have
completed your contract, you will want to get some assurance that
you have in fact learned what you set out to learn. Perhaps the
simplest way to do this is to ask the consultants you used in Step
6 to examine your evidence and validation data and give you their
judgment about their adequacy.

APPENDIX C
Sample Learning Contract (Partial)

Learner: ___Maria Doah___

Learning experience: ___Th. & Prac. of Adult Ed. Methodology___

What are you going to learn? (Objectives)	How are you going to learn it? (Resources and strategies)	Target date for completion	How are you going to know that you learned it? (Evidence)	How are you going to prove that you learned it? (Verification)
1. To develop the ability to describe the differences between youth and adults as learners and the implications for learning and teaching.	Read references cited in Inquiry Unit 1.2. Interview 3 persons from each age group: 6–10, 15–18, 19–22, 23–35, 45–50, 65–70.	Feb. 28	Make a videotape presentation of the differences and their implications.	Have videotape rated on a scale of 0–10 by 3 educational psychologists and 3 experienced teachers. A mean rating of 8.5 will be verification.
2. Skill in designing learning experiences that will accomplish a variety of purposes for several different kinds of learners.	Read references cited in Units 1.2 and 1.3.	March 16	Design (1) a one-day workshop for supervisors on delegating authority; (2) a 10-week course for school dropouts on job hunting; (3) a 20-week course on Understanding the Bible.	Have the designs rated by a supervisory trainer, a vocational educator, and a religious educator in terms of their feasibility, excellence of content, and involvement of learners.
3. Greater ability to select methods, techniques, and materials for accomplishing a variety of educational objectives and explaining my rationale for selecting them.	Read references cited in Units 2.1 and 2.2. Interview 3 experienced trainers in government and industry and 3 experienced teachers in university extension about how they select.	March 30	Indicate methods, techniques, and materials for the designs in (2), and give rationale for selecting them.	Have the 6 persons interviewed critique my selections and rate them in terms of poor, fair, good, excellent. An average of "good" is verification.
4. To increase my skill and confidence in using simulation techniques.	Read references cited in Unit 2.1 that deal with simulation techniques. Attend a workshop sponsored by my ASTD chapter on simulation techniques (I am the program chairperson).	April 15	Do a role-playing, critical-incident, case discussion, and in-basket exercise in a course I teach.	Have my performance rated by my students according to an evaluation form I shall construct.

APPENDIX D
Learning Contract

Learner: _____

Learning experience: _____

What are you going to learn? (Objectives)	How are you going to learn it? (Resources and strategies)	Target date for completion	How are you going to know that you learned it? (Evidence)	How are you going to prove that you learned it? (Verification)

Sample Learning Contract

Learner: __Carl J. Ratcliffe__

Learning experience: __Adult Education: Theory and Practice__

What are you going to learn? (Objectives)	How are you going to learn it? (Resources and strategies)	Target date for completion	How are you going to know that you learned it? (Evidence)	How are you going to prove that you learned it? (Verification)
Unit 1				
1. To evaluate my present learning needs and set objectives for the Theory and Practice of Adult Education Methodology class.	(a) Complete the self-evaluation diagnostic guide in the class text, pages 27–34. (b) Use the counselor competencies lists of Menne and White to assist in making a diagnostic and planning guide (reevaluated from last quarter). (c) *Self-Directed Learning* will be reviewed with emphasis on learning resources B and C.	April 10	Creation of a satisfactory learning contract.	The competencies and the learning contract will be presented to the Nova professor and three other consultants. Each person will receive a card to rate the contract on a scale of 1–10 (a 7.0 average will be acceptable) in depth and practicality of the selected competencies. Comments for modification of the contract will be solicited.
2. To gain a better understanding of the differences between andragogical and pedagogical concepts.	Locate and read as many of the reference articles from Unit 1 as available. Emphasis will be upon the information on the differences between youth and adult educational concepts.	April 10	An article on the differences between youth and adult education will be written.	The article will be critiqued on a scale of 1–10 for comprehensiveness and usefulness by at least four of Calhoun College's faculty members. Reference material will be submitted with the article and critique cards.
Unit 2				
3. To gain a knowledge of computer-assisted education and to understand when using the computer is applicable.	Find and read articles and books on the use of computer-assisted instruction.	May 8	Write an article on the types and appropriate use of computer-assisted instruction.	Have the article critiqued on a scale of 1–10 for comprehensiveness and usefulness by four colleagues. The article, critique, and reference material will be submitted to the Nova lecturer as verification.

Sample Learning Contract, Cont'd.

What are you going to learn? (Objectives)	How are you going to learn it? (Resources and strategies)	Target date for completion	How are you going to know that you learned it? (Evidence)	How are you going to prove that you learned it? (Verification)
4. To increase my understanding of methods or formats for organizing learning experiences.	Read the available references for Unit 2 and other articles on methods or formats.	May 8	Make a list of methods or formats for organizing learning experiences with a brief description of each.	The list will be submitted to three of the Nova consultant group to be rated 1–10 on completeness. The list, critique, and reference material will be submitted to the Nova lecturer as verification.
Unit 3				
5. To develop an understanding of the concept of lifelong learning.	Read available material for Unit 3 and complete note cards on *The Lifelong Learner* by Ronald Gross plus any available articles on lifelong learning.	June 5	Write an article on the basic concepts of lifelong learning.	Have the article read and critiqued by six members of the student development staff for usefulness and clarity on a scale of 1–10. The article and critique will be submitted to the Nova lecturer.
6. To complete videotapes of the nighttime student orientation class to be used for students to make up missed sessions. See: Unit 3.3.2 and 3.8.1 competencies as well as item 9 (Tutoring Techniques) on page 4.	At present, the counselor must schedule a one-hour makeup session for students who miss the information given in student orientation. Videotapes would allow the student to gain the information while leaving the counselor free for other duties.	June 5	Videotape the three one-hour sessions of the night student orientation class.	The videotape will be critiqued by the two other nighttime counselors who present the same program for practicality, depth, and applicability on a scale of 1–10. The critiques will be submitted to the Nova lecturer.

Observations and Reflections

The portfolio of evidence submitted by Carl J. Ratcliffe was outstanding. The article in which he described his learnings for Objective 2 was comprehensive and written in a form suitable for publication. It was evaluated as very useful by four college faculty members. The article for Objective 3 was rated by four other colleagues as so clear and practical that it was recommended for adoption as a manual on computer-assisted instruction by the college. The list of methods and their uses for Objective 4 was comprehensive and imaginative. The article on basic concepts of lifelong learning for Objective 5 was rated near the top of the scale by the student development staff. The videotape of the orientation class for Objective 6 was also rated at the top of the scale and has been used by the college ever since. I agreed with all the ratings.

The four other learners in this seminar submitted contracts with some common objectives (2, 4, 5), but each one had two or more objectives that were geared to that learner's unique needs and interests. Their portfolios of evidence ranged from adequate to superior.

At the beginning of the first session several learners expressed some anxiety about having to take this degree of responsibility for planning their own learning, but the level of anxiety visibly diminished during the review of the contracts by the consultation triads in the morning. Incidentally, I have found that having peers review the contracts before I see them greatly reduces my load in reviewing them. Learners can confront one another in ways that I would not dare do for fear of alienating them. Almost always the contracts are revised and improved during this peer review. But I take responsibility for a final review and often make suggestions for further revision.

I also set the norm that contracts are renegotiable until the end of the seminar, and three learners negotiated revisions at the beginning of the second session—one had discovered from her reading that she needed to add another objective, one had learned about some other resources (content experts) he wanted to add, and the third wanted to make his evidence more rigorous.

Perhaps my most significant observation was the degree of involvement and excitement the learners evidenced when they started to carry out their learning plans and particularly the energy and creativity they exhibited during the team presentations. It was quite common, also, for the teams to build into their presentations opportunities to make use of my content resources.

As I reflected on this experience, I realized that my main psychic reward came from witnessing the release of so much energy for learning.

TWO

How Contract Learning Evolved and How It Works

What Is Contract Learning?

■ *If you look up* contract *in a dictionary, you will find it defined as something like "a binding agreement between two or more persons or parties." That has a rather legalistic feel to it, and so some people prefer to call learning contracts "learning plans" or "learning agreements" or "study plans" or "self-development plans." But if you want to find out what has been written about it in the literature, the most productive term to search for would be* contract learning *or* learning contracts.

A learning contract typically specifies (1) the knowledge, skills, attitudes, and values to be acquired by the learner (learning objectives), (2) how these objectives are to be accomplished (learning resources and strategies), (3) the target date for their accomplishment, (4) what evidence will be presented to demonstrate that the objectives have been accomplished, and (5) how this evidence will be judged or validated. In academic settings the contract often also specifies what grade is sought.

The contract may be between a learner and himself or herself; it may be between an individual learner or group of learners and an instructor or mentor; it may be between a worker and a supervisor or manager; or it may be between an individual and a group (such as a faculty committee or a staff-development committee).

The contract may have as its purpose the accomplishment of the objectives of particular units or projects of a course or of a whole course, of a staff-development program, of a clinical experience or internship, of a total degree program, or of a personal development project. Examples of each of these purposes are presented in this book. But contract learning is such a flexible concept that it is practically impossible to organize it into a definitive classification system. One

38

possible classification would be according to the source of objectives. In this book there are three examples (Selections 3, 10, 19) in which the objectives are prescribed by the instructor or the institution, leaving for the learners only a choice of strategies for accomplishing the objectives. Three of the selections (1, 11, 13) present predetermined options from which the students may choose. All other selections provide for some input from the learners regarding the objectives, ranging from minimal input to total freedom subject to agreement by the instructor. Some selections (12, 13, 14) provide for the learners to specify what grade they want to contract for. Most of the selections, however, provide for some other method of assigning grades.

New College at the University of South Florida has developed a typology of seven categories of contracts to provide learners and their sponsors with a variety of options, as follows:

Survey contract: *An examination of the content of various fields of knowledge.*

Methodological contract: *An exploration of the techniques and modes of thought characteristic of one or more disciplines.*

Thematic contract: *An exploration of different subject matter that possesses thematic focus.*

Research contract: *An in-depth study of a problem that requires extensive work in either the laboratory or the field.*

Skill contract: *The acquisition of skills in fields such as the studio or performing arts or a foreign language.*

Applied contract: *An attempted integration of classroom and field experience or of theory and practice.*

Off-campus study contract: *Study at another college or university, research at specialized institutes, an internship, or a field experience project.*

The selections in this book are organized according to the context in which the contracting is done: in independent study (Chapter Four), in academic classroom courses (Chapter Five), in clinical courses, graduate assistantships, and internships (Chapter Six), in continuing professional and management development (Chapter Seven), and in total degree programs (Chapter Eight). In the introduction to each selection, features that are "of special interest" are identified in order to help the reader choose those selections that will be most useful.

Contract learning is, in essence, an alternative way of structuring a learning experience: It replaces a content plan with a process plan. Instead of specifying how a body of content will be transmitted (content *plan), it specifies how a body of content will be acquired by the learner (process plan).*

What Are the Theoretical/Philosophical Foundations of Contract Learning?

The conceptual roots of contract learning probably go back to the theory and practice of independent study, starting in the early 1920s (Dressel and Thompson, 1973, p. 2), which, in turn, was stimulated by the philosophy of John Dewey. The basic premise of independent study is that "the ability to carry on independent study alone or with peers should be a major goal of education" (Dressel and Thompson, p. 2). These authors define independent study as "the student's self-directed pursuit of academic competence in as autonomous a manner as he is able to exercise at any particular time" (p. 1). They go on to explain, "We prefer the term independent study *as describing an ability to be developed in some measure in every student. It means motivation, curiosity, a sense of self-sufficiency and self-direction, ability to think critically and creatively, awareness of resources, and some ability to use them" (p. 7). They conclude by pointing to "the desirability of encouraging every student from the time of his arrival on campus to become a self-directed learner, combining this self-direction when appropriate with the advantageous sharing of this experience with his peer group. Indeed, it seems reasonable to argue that no student should receive a baccalaureate degree who has not demonstrated his capacity to operate in this manner" (p. 11).*

This conceptual base became enriched in the 1960s with experimentation and research in the individualization of instruction. Researchers such as Bloom (1968), McKeachie (1963), and Minter (1967) proposed that instruction should be suited to students' individual differences and goals. Summarizing these research findings, Siegel (1968, p. 149) concluded that "to be most effective, instruction must be tailored to the needs, capabilities, and histories of the individual learners."

Further enrichment took place during the 1960s and later with a flood of research and theorizing on self-directed learning (Boud, 1981; Cross, 1976, 1981; Houle, 1961; Knowles, 1975; Rogers, 1969; Tough, 1967, 1979) and on lifelong learning (Boshier, 1980; Botkin, Elmandjra, and Malitza, 1979; Cropley, 1980; Dave, 1975; Faure and others, 1972; Gross, 1977). A strong theme running through this literature is that our entire educational enterprise should be organized around the concept of lifelong learning, with the primary mission of schooling to be the development of skills of self-directed learning.

In the late 1960s and early 1970s there appeared in the literature a conceptual model of learning and instruction that incorporates the concepts of independent study, individualized instruction, and self-directed and lifelong learning into a comprehensive theoretical framework. It was labeled "andragogy," meaning the art and science of helping adults learn (later extended to the art and science of helping people learn). Contract learning is an approach to education that is most congruent with the assumptions about learners on which the andragogical model is based (Ingalls and Arceri, 1972; Knowles, 1975, 1980, 1984; Knowles and Associates, 1984), which are as follows:

1. The need to know. Learners need to understand the need to learn something—how it will benefit them if they learn it or what the consequences will be if they do not—before they are willing to invest time and energy in learning it (Houle, 1972; Tough, 1979). In the process of drafting a learning contract, learners are subtly challenged to think through why they are undertaking to learn something.

2. The need to be self-directing. The psychological definition of adult is "one who has achieved a self-concept of being responsible for himself or herself—whose self-perception is that of a self-directing person." And when a person has arrived at that self-concept, he or she experiences a deep psychological need to be seen by others and treated by others as being capable of being self-directing. Contract learning at its best involves the learners in making decisions about what will be learned, how it will be learned, when it will be learned, and whether it has been learned, usually with the help of a facilitator or resource person.

3. The need to have the learners' unique experiences taken into account. It is predictable that in a group of adults the range of experience, both in quantity and in quality, will be greater than in a group of children. Because of their experience, adults have developed different styles of learning, different levels of operation, different needs and interests, different speeds of learning, and different patterns of thought. Hence the importance, particularly with adults, of providing for highly individualized plans for learning. Learning contracts are almost always individualized plans for learning. Five individuals may have the same objective in their contracts and go about accomplishing that objective in five different ways.

4. The need to gear learning to the learners' readiness to learn. Adults become ready to learn something when they experience in their life situation a need to learn it. Since the life situations of any group of adults are different, they become ready to learn different things at different times. Learning contracts provide the flexibility to enable different learners to time their learning according to their readiness to learn.

5. The need to organize learning around life tasks or life problems. *Adults have a task-centered or problem-centered orientation to learning, rather than the subject-centered orientation that is characteristic of children. Learning contracts enable learners to state their objectives in terms of tasks or problems that are related to their life situations.*

6. The need to tap into intrinsic motivations. *Children and youth have been conditioned by their school experience to rely on extrinsic motivators—pressure from parents, teachers, and the grading system. Although adults respond to some extent to extrinsic motivators (wage increases, job promotions), their deepest motivation comes from such intrinsic motivators as increases in self-esteem, responsibility, creativity, and self-fulfillment. Learning contracts challenge learners to tap into the intrinsic motivators.*

At some time, some innovative instructor must have started using learning contracts—probably initially in the form of a simple written agreement between an independent study mentor and a learner. The word must have spread that it was an effective way to structure learning, so that today contract learning is used pervasively enough to make this book possible.

Where and When Is Contract Learning Used?

Institutions of higher education are, without doubt, currently the most prolific users of contract learning. It is the predominant mode in most external degree programs, as illustrated in Chapter Eight, and in independent study courses, as illustrated in Chapter Four. It is used extensively in clinical placements (Chapters Three and Six), professional courses (Chapters One and Three), and continuing professional and management development programs (Chapter Seven). It is coming into increasing use even in academic classroom courses, usually for particular units or projects but often for entire courses (Chapter Five).

But it is being used increasingly in staff development programs in business and industry (Knowles, 1984; Knowles and Associates, 1984), health agencies (Knowles and Associates, 1984), government agencies (Ingalls and Arceri, 1972; Knowles and Associates, 1984). I have had some reports of its being used in elementary and secondary schools (Knowles and Associates, 1984). Perhaps it is also being used in other institutional settings, such as voluntary organizations, but I have no information about this.

My impression is that it is the method of choice when regular courses are not available in a particular subject, when learners cannot attend campus-based courses, when the desired learning objectives cut across disciplines, when there is a wide range of differences among learners, and when instructors or institutions have a commitment to develop the skills of self-directed learning.

It appears not to be an effective method—or at least a method of choice—in situations involving the development of precise psychomotor skills (machine operation, surgical procedures), human relations skills that require interaction in groups, or subject matter that is entirely strange to the learners. It presents special problems when the learners are deeply dependent (see "Observations and Reflections" in Chapter Four).

In the early stages of the development of independent study programs, the assumption was made that it was appropriate only for superior students. But Baskin (1962, p. 51) points out that "although independent study has been thought of most often as a release of the swift and able learner from bondage to a plodding pace, permitting him to leap ahead with joy, it may equally be thought of as an emancipation of the slower but still respectable learner from a dizzying pace that leaves him baffled and defeated." And Gruber and Weitman's study (1962, pp. 23–28) of academic ability and self-directed study finds "little or no support for the notion of a direct relation between intellectual ability and capacity to profit from self-directed study." If we accept the proposition that the primary mission of education should be to develop the skills of self-directed learning, then presumably we should make contract learning available to all learners and find ways to give special help to those who find it difficult.

How Is It Done?

That is the question, of course, that this whole book addresses. There is no one right way. In fact, one of the chief virtues of contract learning is its almost infinite flexibility. Its heart is the process of negotiation between learners, facilitators, and resource persons. The process used in various situations is described in all selections, and guidelines for learners are reproduced in Selections 1, 5, 7, 14, 16, and 22.

What Are the Roles of Instructors and Learners?

In essence, in contract learning the role of the instructor shifts from that of a didactic transmitter of content and controller of learners to that of a facilitator of self-directed learning and content resource (or broker). When I made the transition from didactic teacher to facilitator of learning, I found three adjustments to be critical. First, I had to construct an intellectual model of the role of facilitator for myself, and in this regard I found the existing models of counselor and consultant most useful. Then I had to identify the skills that would be required in the new role and develop them—again, essentially the skills of the counselor and consultant. And, finally, I had to experience the greater psychic rewards that come from releasing rather than controlling the energy of learners and change my value system accordingly.

The role of the learner shifts from that of more or less passive receiver of transmitted information and submissive executor of the instructor's directives to that of initiative-taking planner and executor of strategies and resources for achieving mutually agreed-on objectives. The relationship between the two parties is one of colleagues and mutual learners. In most academic situations the instructor is ultimately accountable to the institution, and so he or she must accept ultimate responsibility for the quality of the learning. But if the nature and boundaries of this responsibility and the criteria for implementing it are described explicitly from the outset, it need not interfere with the relationship of mutuality. In my own practice I make it clear that evaluation is a factor in the negotiation process.

A clear statement of "The Role and Responsibilities of Persons Working with Learning Contracts" appears in Whatcom Community College's Study Guide for Personal Educational Planning. Whatcom also makes use of a "broker," as described in Selection 5. Here is the statement:

Student

1. *Propose a written learning contract of what and how you want to learn.*
2. *Set up a time line or schedule that allows you to work on the learning contract activities each week.*
3. *If you are having problems with the learning contract, are stuck and need motivation, need information, or want feedback on how you are doing, contact your mentor immediately. Take the initiative to get assistance when you need it.*
4. *Meet with your mentor regularly. Call to make an appointment.*

Mentor

1. *Review or assist in developing the student's learning contract to ensure that it is complete and of good quality.*
2. *Recommend learning resources—books, journals, people, agencies, and so on.*
3. *Be a resource for information but do not assume the responsibility for "teaching" the student.*

4. Meet regularly with the student to review progress, share ideas, and motivate.
5. Evaluate the student's work as described in the learning contract.
6. Report the final grade (usually "pass" or "fail") to Registration or the Alternative Learning Experiences Office.
7. Keep track and report all time spent with the learning contract to the broker.

Broker

1. Inform the student of the learning contract process, policies, and procedures.
2. Determine the most appropriate mentor for each contract and link the mentor with the student.
3. Inform the mentor about the learning contract policies and procedures.
4. Problem-solve appropriate situations that arise.
5. Process the hiring, faculty contract, and payroll for mentors.
6. Suggest learning resources.
7. Ensure quality control for learning contracts.

Speaking from my personal experience, I find that the most critical points in the contracting process, those that require most of my time and effort, are these: (1) Orienting the learners to the processes of self-directed and contract learning. I do this both through group activities and through individual coaching. (2) Negotiating the learning contract. I insist that the learners prepare the first draft. Then I have the contracts reviewed in peer groups of three or four (incidentally, I find that peers can be much more confronting about sloppy work than I would dare be). Then I review the contracts individually, give my reactions, and negotiate differences. I have found that it is crucial that I not accept a contract until it meets agreed-on standards. (3) Providing psychic support and resource information and monitoring progress while the contracts are being carried out. (4) Evaluating the evidence of accomplishment of the objectives of the contract. Here again, I feel responsible for assuring that the evidence specified in the contract is contained in the portfolio of evidence and, if it is not, for negotiating with the learner for its inclusion.

I find that I can serve as many students as a contract learning mentor as I did as a didactic teacher; I simply use my time and energy differently.

What Are Its Benefits and Limitations?

Contract learning yields many practical benefits:

■ *It gets the learners more ego-involved in their own learning; it "turns them on" to learning. Once they pass through the stage of confusion and anxiety that they typically experience as they start to do it for the first time, they get excited about carrying out their own plans. In my experience, learners will invest more energy in learning what they have been involved in planning than I would dare to require of them as a didactic teacher.*

■ *It causes them to make use of a much wider variety of resources for learning, such as peers, other people in the institution and community, field experiences, and the like, thus lessening the load typically carried by instructors who see themselves as the only resources available.*

■ *It sharpens learners' skills of self-directed learning, thus giving them a tool that will enhance their ability to learn from their experience and their environment for the rest of their lives.*

■ *It increases the accountability of the program by providing more functional and validated evidence of the learning outcomes.*

■ *It provides a more functional way of structuring learning—a process structure in the place of the traditional content-transmission structure.*

■ *It replaces the conventional teacher-imposed discipline with self-discipline in the learning process.*

■ *It provides a way for the learner to obtain continual feedback about progress being made toward accomplishing learning goals.*

■ *It is more cost-effective than traditional teacher-directed learning, in that the learner is less dependent on exclusive use of the resources of instructors and takes some of the responsibility for directing the learning off their shoulders.*

Contract learning adds to the quality of learning because it involves learners in taking responsibility, with the help of a mentor or resource person, for planning and carrying out their own learning. A basic law of human nature is at work here: People tend to feel committed to a decision or activity in proportion to the extent that they feel they have participated in making the decision or planning the activity. The reverse is even more true: People tend to feel uncommitted to a decision or activity in proportion to the extent that they feel the decision or activity is being imposed on them by others.

But contract learning also has some limitations:

■ *It is not suitable for all situations, such as those involving development of psychomotor or interpersonal skills and those involving the acquisition of content with which learners are totally unfamiliar.*

■ *It poses special problems for learners who have dependent personalities.*

■ *It requires a reorientation to learning by learners who are highly self-directing in all other aspects of their lives.*

■ *It is most effective when there is strong institutional support for it—a characteristic not present in many traditional institutions.*

■ *It requires that teachers redefine their roles and adopt a different system of psychic rewards.*

THREE

Introducing Contract Learning in an Organization or Program

■ *The notion of introducing contract learning into a total system—a course, a department, a school, an organization, particularly in a traditional institution—can be frightening. What if people are not ready for it? What if learners cannot do it? What if faculty or students rebel? What if it fails? What will happen to our traditions, rules and regulations, and standards?*

My own starting point, as I explain in the Preface, was with small units or projects of particular courses, the learners having the option of participating in the experiment or not. Then, as the learners and I became secure with the process, I expanded it gradually to whole courses and, eventually, total degree programs. A few institutions of recent origin—such as New College of the University of Alabama, New College of the University of West Florida, Empire State College, and the School of Lifelong Learning of the University of New Hampshire system—used contract learning from their inception as an integral part of their way of operating. But they also took special care to orient the learners and faculty to the process in advance of their starting with it.

The selections in this chapter describe how contract learning was introduced in three professional schools with long traditions of didactic instruction. One of the authors told me, "If it can be done in my university, it can be done anywhere."

Selection Two presents the experience of the Department of Social Work at the University of North Dakota in introducing contract learning into the field placement program. It first makes a case for the special relevance of contract learning for social work education and then describes what went wrong when it was introduced by faculty imposition and how it succeeded when introduced in small increments—for a term paper in a human behavior course and one unit of a methods course—before being used in field placements. Examples of the three types of contracts are exhibited. This selection was prepared expressly for this book by Leola Furman, Myrna Hagg, and Thomasein Heitcamp, faculty members in the Department of Social Work at the University of North Dakota.

Selection Three gives a detailed description of the use of contract learning in clinical nursing placements at Capital University in Columbus, Ohio. It opens with an overview of the changing picture in higher education that necessitates a more individualized approach to learning. It then describes how contract learning was given trial runs with two groups of learners before being adopted for the clinical course, how learners were oriented to the contracting process before starting with it, how the contracts were developed, how the time required for developing contracts was reduced with experience, how progress was monitored, and what policies for grading were. A special bonus is a report of an evaluation of the experience by learners and faculty, followed by a helpful discussion of "Considerations, Drawbacks, and Merits." A sample contract is shown. This selection is reproduced with permission from "Self-Directed Learning: An Option for Nursing Education," by Karen Martens, R.N., in Nursing Outlook, August 1981, pp. 472–475. Karen Martens is assistant professor of nursing at Capital University.

Selection Four is an example of the use of contracts for an "Adulthood and Aging" course at the Quillen-Dishner College of Medicine, East Tennessee State University. The procedures used and author are described in the introduction to the selection.

■SELECTION 2

A Case History: Introducing Contract Learning at the Department of Social Work, University of North Dakota

Learning contracts are a valuable tool for providing instruction in basic social work values, skills, and knowledge. The profession of social work recognizes the importance of every individual's right to self-determination, respect, dignity, and worth. Social work requires that its instructors exemplify a humanistic approach to instruction and serve as role models for the learners.

Learning contracts are also a tool that allows students to focus on their strengths and interests and gear their learning to their individual learning styles and needs—other concepts that are transferable to practice with our client population. This type of instruction encourages self-responsibility and creative problem solving—valuable assets in pursuing their academic and professional careers.

The faculty of the University of North Dakota Department of Social Work was exposed to the idea of contract learning when Malcolm Knowles conducted a faculty-development workshop there in the fall of 1983. The field coordinator and faculty liaison had both utilized learning contracts for their own continuing professional development but had not used them in their teaching. As a result of the Knowles workshop, they decided to request that the students complete a learning contract for their field placement.

The plan was put into action when the students returned to campus for their midsemester integrative seminar. They were given a one-hour lecture, with discussion, on contract learning and then were told to construct a contract. It was an order! The students exploded with anger. They made remarks such as "The university is Mickey Mouse; it's not teaching me." The backlash from the students was so severe that the requirement was rescinded.

The coordinator and liaison then reviewed Boud (1981), Gibbs (1977), and Kelly (1955), all of whom pointed out that new educational procedures need to be introduced gradually and through a process of negotiation with the students. The instructors regrouped and decided that they were not willing to abandon the idea of contract learning.

One of the instructors consulted with Malcolm Knowles, who suggested that we try inviting students to develop contracts for a single unit or term paper in courses prior to their field placement. Accordingly, students were introduced to contract learning in the course "Human Behavior in the Social Environment" before entering into their field practicum. They were given the option of constructing a contract for the term paper in that course. Exhibit 1 is an example of a term-paper contract.

The next level of contracting occurred in the Methods II course, which was completed before the student entered the field instruction. This course was designed to develop interviewing and counseling skills. Students were videotaped conducting interviews and then assessed their strengths and weaknesses by viewing themselves on playback monitors. They then constructed a learning contract to enhance their interviewing skills. This contract was presented to their clinical instructors at initial interviews with them. Exhibit 2 is an example of this contract.

A clinical site was selected in consultation with the faculty adviser, and a learning contract was negotiated by the student with the clinical instructor and faculty liaison. Although the student took the initiative in developing a contract, the faculty representatives had to assure that necessary academic requirements were satisfied. Exhibit 3 is an example of a field placement contract.

Exhibit 1. Learning Contract for a Term Paper.

Learner _____ Learning experience _Term paper for Human Behavior_

What are you going to learn? (objectives) Knowledge concerning:	How are you going to learn it? (resources and strategies)	Target date for completion	How are you going to know that you learned it? (evidence)	How are you going to prove that you learned it? (verification by judges)
A. Centuries of elderly 1. Different countries' views on the elderly 2. Early American treatment of elderly 3. Medical information re aging	Library books Interlibrary connections History books	May 12–25	1. The written term paper 2. Discussion of each topic with my judging panel 3. Possible oral presentation 4. Ability to communicate with the elderly population 5. Effective performance at an agency for the elderly	1. Social work instructor 2. Composition content by English instructor 3. Evaluation by agency peers 4. Aging content by sociology instructor

B. Endurance of the elderly	1. Interviews:
	  a. Ombudsmen in nursing homes
	  b. Individuals I know
	2. Library magazines
		May 26–June 8		

C. Tolerance toward the elderly	Interviews: ■ Ombudsman program ■ Helping agencies ■ General public ■ Observations in travels	June 9–22		
D. The family and the elderly	Library books, journals, interviews, magazines	June 23–July 6		
E. Homes for the elderly 1. Institutions 2. Rent or own? 3. Retirement communities 4. Shared housing	Interviews, books, journals, lectures, observations	July 7–20		

Exhibit 2. Learning Contract for a Unit of a Course.

Learner _____   Unit of a course: Methods II—interviewing skills
                              Learning experience _____

What are you going to learn? (objectives)	How are you going to learn it? (resources and strategies)	Target date for completion	How are you going to know that you learned it? (evidence)	How are you going to prove that you learned it? (verification by judges)
To gain more confidence and become more relaxed when interviewing	By role-playing feedback from supervisor and co-workers	July 31	By my own self-assessment. By the verbal and nonverbal responses of the clients	By videotaping at the beginning of the internship and at the conclusion and comparing by supervisor and co-workers
To improve the flow of the interview	By studying and practicing various concepts of interviewing and videotaping role playing of interviews	July 31	By self-evaluation of videotapes. By the way a client reacts to me	By evaluation of supervisor
To become more knowledgeable about family therapy	By reading material about various therapy models—Satir, Minuchin, Haley	July 31	By writing a short paper about various models. By being capable of using the various models in role playing. By being able to discuss the models comfortably with co-workers and supervisors	By evaluation of my supervisors on my use and knowledge of these models

Exhibit 3. Learning Contract for Field Placement.

Learner _____

Field placement in an agency serving Native Americans

Learning experience _____

What are you going to learn? (objectives)	How are you going to learn it? (resources and strategies)	Target date for completion	How are you going to know that you learned it? (evidence)	How are you going to prove that you learned it? (verification by judges)
To become knowledgeable about the agency and its programs	Interview staff members re their roles Read available literature on the programs Attend staff, area head, and in-service meetings	Feb. 11	Observation of a student taking action or understanding a concept through my assistance	Report on the agency at the Integrative Seminar, with feedback
To become familiar with the Native American culture	Research written and recorded material on Native American culture Attend Native American cultural events Interview Native Americans	Ongoing	Make a presentation to a Native American group	Ask them to evaluate its accuracy and comprehensiveness
To feel more comfortable in working with and in front of groups of people	Begin working with small groups of 3 or 4 persons, then increasing numbers as comfort increases	May 3	I feel decreasing anxiety Response of the group My ability to volunteer for group leadership or presentations	Verbal feedback from observers (counselors, students, staff) Critique from those involved
To improve on the social work skills learned in Methods I and II	Prepare a list of social work skills prior to meetings with clients, then evaluate afterwards as to what skills were used and the degree of effectiveness of each	May 3	Response from clients in interviews or sessions Feedback from co-workers, staff members	Evaluation of contact sheets by supervisor Role play a client interview with supervisor and get evaluation of my skills

■ SELECTION 3

Introducing Contract Learning into Clinical Nursing Placements at Capital University

Changing enrollment patterns and student expectations have inspired many nursing faculty members to reevaluate their course content and teaching methods. Innovative techniques are needed to help generic students polish their skills and prepare for the reality of their first job, while R.N. students need freedom, with guidance, to build upon past experiences rather than to repeat them. Although the ratio of faculty to students has increased at many schools, students' demands to explore more varied aspects of practice and develop a broader professional perspective are greater than ever. Many programs offer students the opportunity to learn in a one-to-one relationship with a nurse preceptor who is an affiliating agency employee (Chickerella and Lutz, 1981).

It has become commonplace to consider the importance of encouraging people to take increased responsibility for their own health. The developmental importance of permitting students to assume responsibility for their own learning is analogous. Indeed, the major responsibility for learning does belong to the student (Asteriadis, 1976). Self-directed learning, as approached by Knowles (1975), offers one tool for increased self-responsibility in learning.

Recently, this methodological design has been used in the final nursing course at Capital University. The student determines what she wants to accomplish in the clinical component of the course and then translates it into a written contract identifying (1) learning objectives, (2) resources and strategies for learning, (3) evidence of accomplishment, and (4) criteria for evaluation. Students learn in a one-to-one relationship with a nurse preceptor who provides daily clinical guidance. Each student's placement within an agency is determined by considering the type of clinical experience the student desires.

Contract Development

While the literature reports use of teacher-constructed contracts and recommends the use of contracts in the clinical area, Knowles's approach had not previously been used in nursing education. After the successful trial experiences of two small groups of students with learning contracts, faculty members decided to make self-directed learning an integral part of the course "Professional Term."

The concepts and principles of self-directed learning were introduced in the opening classes of the course. Informational materials were distributed, and large- and small-group discussions were held. To further understanding of the concept, Knowles's (1975) *Self-Directed Learning* was used as a reference to help students understand the process of writing the contract. In addition, examples of previously written contracts were distributed in class, and a recent graduate spoke about her experience with this process.

Development of each student's contract took place over the next two to three weeks. Students' reactions, as they began the process, were interesting. Some were already aware of their learning needs and quickly formulated relevant objectives. Others were unsure of personal goals and what we were asking of them. Obviously, there was a need for the student to use many resources during the contract development period. Conferences between faculty members and individual students helped refine definitions of learning needs. Preceptors familiarized the student with available learning opportunities in the clinical settings.

Creative Writing

Not only were students expected to determine their own specific learning objectives in the first part of the contract, but their individual objectives would also have to meet the more general course objectives. Thus, a certain amount of synthesis was required to write an acceptable contract. However, individuality and variety of learning objectives would be more feasible in this course than others, since course content was designed to integrate and incorporate theory and practice already learned.

Contract objectives would center around experiences available at the clinical placement agency and would demand leadership, communication, and technical skills; provision of nursing care to groups of people; assertiveness; nursing care related to specific types of illnesses; and patient education. Objectives that necessitated activities outside the placement agency or in departments other than that to which they were assigned for clinical experience would also be permissible. For example, a student wanting to increase her knowledge of psychotherapy of adolescents might plan for a three-day experience at a drug rehabilitation agency to observe and actively participate in the group session. Another student might request placement in a cardiac care unit but could also visit both the local chapter of the American Heart Association and a cardiac rehabilitation facility to help her better understand community resources available for education and rehabilitation.

The second section of the learning contract demands identification of the various resources and strategies the student intends to use to accomplish each objective. Such resources might include specific literature, activities, observations, field trips, and the like. As students became more enthusiastically imaginative, this section quickly became filled with meaningful strategies.

The third and fourth sections of the contract contain closely related information—evidence of accomplishment and criteria and means of evaluating that evidence. Initially, many students find it difficult to differentiate between these two sections. Evidence of accomplishment asks students to list activities that will convince themselves and others that their objectives were achieved. The intent of section four, criteria and means of validating, is to have the students specify how that evidence is to be evaluated.

Contract Mechanics

The amount of time students needed to develop the contract ranged from three to seventy-six hours over a three-week period with most students spending between ten and twenty hours. The period of contract development has been successfully shortened in subsequent courses, as the course structure changed to an eight-week module. The contracts, however, are developed as well as, if not better than, they were with more time.

When the contract is acceptable to the student, clinical preceptor, and faculty member, all three sign the contract. Renegotiation for unforeseen changes is permitted until midsemester. Active use of the contract throughout the semester is essential since the contract must be used as the working tool it is intended to be. Periodic review of the progress being made in fulfilling the contract is beneficial. This review seems most successful when done in a three-way conference between student, preceptor, and faculty member. In addition to assessing the student's progress, these conferences alert all parties to any needed input from faculty member or preceptor, which the student may require to meet her objectives.

The written contract is the basis for later evaluation of the clinical performance, and it constitutes 40 percent of the course grade. Development of the contract is another 15 percent of the grade. Other components of the final course grade include student presentations, written exams, and a term paper.

Evaluation of clinical learning is accomplished by determining the extent to which the contract is fulfilled. We decided to give full credit for the clinical portion of the course grade if the student completed all she had set out to do as stated in her contract. The few situations in which contracts were incompletely fulfilled were dealt with by proportionate reduction in grade. For instance, if a student having ten objectives failed to meet one of the objectives, 10 percent of the clinical grade was deducted from the student's final grade. The majority of students fulfilled all contract requirements.

Asking for Comments

To evaluate this self-directed approach to learning, two questionnaires were developed. One was given to the students and the other to the preceptors.

The responses to both questionnaires were supportive of self-directed learning. Forty students (55 percent) and fifty-three preceptors (74 percent) responded. Of the students, thirty-four indicated satisfaction in developing a learning contract, and thirty-eight stated that the learning contract helped to clarify their learning needs. Only four students felt that development of the contract required too much time. Thirty-three students stated that the contract gave them a sense of greater control of their own learning, and thirty-eight (95 percent) said the contract helped them articulate their needs to their preceptors.

Many of the comments offered about the contract development period demonstrated the importance of giving the students specific guidelines and/or providing them with adequate guidance from faculty. Several mentioned contract examples as being important. One person wrote:

> Since this was a new experience, it was frustrating to do for the first time. Even though I knew what to do, exactly how to do it was unclear. The only thing that may help is to explain the concept and help individuals identify personal needs to include in the contract.

The questionnaires also asked about use of the contract, once it was developed. Thirty-nine students found the contract helpful by keeping them focused on their goals; thirty-six used the contract frequently themselves; twenty felt their preceptors frequently used it; and thirty felt their instructors frequently used it. Thirty-seven said the objectives they had written proved to be realistic. Only six found later need for renegotiation. Thirty-four were proud of having developed the contract. Comments from students included:

> This is something I would be proud to show an employer in order to show my learning capabilities, what things I accomplished at the end of school, and my own organizational skills. The advantages of the experience of developing and using the contract are not seen immediately. It is frustrating at first, but by the end of the semester the advantages show up. It was different and I liked the independence I felt.

Most preceptors stated the learning contract helped them plan for student experiences, seemed to be useful for the student, and was clearly stated. Only five thought it seemed a waste of time.

Students generally were positive about self-directed learning, as thirty-five said it encouraged them to learn, and thirty-one said it is a tool they will use in the future. The majority of the students said self-directed learning increased the responsibility they felt for clinical learning. Among the comments offered by students were:

> I felt everything I did was to my own advantage and enabled me to learn at my own pace with deadlines I set and without the usual stress felt in other nursing courses. It's a way of feeling a part of your own learning and really wanting to do it.

> It was difficult for me at first because I had no real role model. I became frustrated at first but with guidance from my instructor, I worked through that. . . . good idea for this semester because this type of learning will be used the rest of my life.

> Excellent concept but such a change from previous learning experiences.

> Made me think for myself. I wanted the instructors to do all the work, but after I did it, I was satisfied with the outcome. It was an achievement I enjoyed.

> This should be taught earlier in the nursing program.

Considerations, Drawbacks, and Merits

Most students being introduced to this concept for the first time require thorough explanations and examples. While the students were offered many discussion periods and adequate time to understand the process, many students stated they would have found the distribution of sample contracts helpful. Although each faculty person in the course had sample contracts that he or she shared with individual students during development conferences, individual copies were not distributed to students. At first it was feared that creativity would be inhibited if contract examples were heavily relied upon, but this does not seem a justifiable reason for withholding them. For the student new to this process, seeing a contract example quickly clears the muddy waters.

Preexisting course objectives might be viewed by some as too restrictive for self-directed learning. It must be recognized, however, that course objectives are not only legitimate in this process but are certainly a necessary measure of achievement in any course. Most nursing course objectives are usually achievable through a variety of activities and often in a variety of settings; it is possible to reach the same destination by different routes. In one's enthusiasm for encouraging individuality and creativity in the student, however, the teacher must assure a fit between the student's individual objectives and course objectives.

Closely related to the issue of course objectives is grading. Whereas we felt justified in giving full credit for the clinical portion of the grade if the student met all the objectives in the learning contract, another approach could also be considered. Grading criteria could be identified during the contract development period to permit each student to evaluate the grade level her contract objectives attained. Assuming that course objectives identify learning that must take place for minimal achievement in any course, the successful completion of the contract could earn the student credit in an average grade range. Students who developed contracts exceeding minimal requirements could earn a higher grade.

Obviously, both approaches to grading have their drawbacks. To define the differences between letter grades would require much time and effort; it would be essential to unify all faculty members' expectations and judgments. That is a most difficult goal to achieve, if it is indeed achievable. Yet, if one gives full credit as we did, is it fair to the student who excels? Ideally, learning efforts are not tied to a grade. Yet, despite the position on grading by this faculty, it is clear that if one grades clinical learning by means of contract fulfillment, all available options need to be thoroughly analyzed and weighed before any approach is chosen.

The expectation of nursing faculty that their students retain and build upon essential knowledge or skill acquired in past courses may also give rise to problems. For example, one faculty member recognized that one of her students was repeatedly breaking aseptic technique. While none of that student's contract objectives directly dealt with this area of nursing practice, the instructor, nevertheless, believed that she was justified in expecting competence in this skill from the student. Possibly sterile technique could have been included as part of an objective relating to nursing process. However, if "nursing process" is not interpreted in the same way by the student and faculty, how can a teacher deal fairly with such a situation after having entered into a contract? Does the student always know what is essential knowledge? Can one expect faculty members to overlook what is not directly specified in the students' contract? Undoubtedly, there are many areas of essential knowledge that senior nursing students ready for graduation would be expected to possess. One approach to this potential dilemma might be a clear explanation to students regarding expectations of past learning. If a deficiency is identified, the student should be made aware of unsatisfactory performance and given the opportunity to correct it.

Self-directed learning seems more applicable to upper-division nursing courses than it does to fundamental courses. As the student approaches graduation, she is more comfortable in the role of the nurse and the various settings in which nurses practice. This comfort and insight enable the student to better realize learning possibilities and the vast array of learning resources. Lower-division courses might introduce the process in selective areas of study to lessen confusion about self-directed learning in later courses.

R.N. students seem to find this approach to learning very useful. Self-directed learning allows the R.N. to build upon past experiences and design further learning with an individual approach. For example, one student interested in patient education worked with a nurse preceptor in a hospital patient-education department. The student designed a contract that included direct teaching, as well as development of a teaching tool to be used for persons admitted to the newly opened same-day surgery unit. By completing the contract, the student gained much experience in a nursing role that was new to her.

It is imperative for a teaching team to clearly understand the self-directed teaching approach and to act consistently in their expectations of students with respect to the contract. Not only is this helpful to students, it is reassuring to faculty members new to this approach to clinical learning. Meetings of the teaching team and discussions of individual teachers' involvement in the process of self-directed learning provide continuity in instructors' approaches to students.

Future Considerations

Today with increasing student-teacher ratios, it is impossible for nursing educators to directly guide and supervise each learning activity for each student. Self-directed learning enables teachers to make learning more creative and satisfying for greater numbers of students, while making teaching more creative and enjoyable for themselves. Faculty members in our course found self-directed learning interesting and challenging. It provided a spark of uniqueness and creativity to their teaching. While some problem areas had to be worked through, all felt it was a worthwhile and effective process.

As our survey showed, students did gain by playing a more active role in their own learning, and in a profession that is constantly evolving and confronting change, any nurse capable of being self-directed in continual professional growth will be an asset.

Sample Student Contract

Learning Objectives	Learning Resources and Strategies	Evidence of Accomplishment	Criteria and Means of Validating Evidence
1. To become more assertive and self-confident	■ Nursing literature ■ *Nursing 78*, January ■ Develop rating scale for measuring self-growth	■ Showing assertive behavior patterns ■ Daily log entries relating to attempts at practicing assertiveness	■ Rating of behavior with use of rating scale by preceptor at the beginning, middle, and end of semester ■ Rating by peers and self of assertive behavior as seen in seminar
2. To gain skill in performing procedures used in step-down CCU	■ Nursing skill books ■ Observation of preceptor and other staff members ■ Reviewing unfamiliar procedures in the policy and procedure manual ■ Nursing literature ■ In-service classes on Code Blue, Crash Cart, Catheter Care ■ Development of checklist for evaluation	■ Have preceptor and other staff members observe procedures and comment on my technique and performance ■ Log entries of procedures performed, how I felt doing it, and any comments, remarks, or corrections for performing the procedure in the future	■ Do final evaluation procedures for the in-services ■ Performance of skills on unit as rated by preceptor or staff with use of rating scale
3. To gain knowledge and understanding of the pathophysiology of the cardiac patient	■ Ask questions while accompanying physicians on rounds ■ Reading and studying charts ■ Attending in-services on cardiac disorders ■ Nursing literature	■ Written care plan each month on different cardiac patients ■ Ability in report to communicate essential information about cardiac patients ■ Placement of pertinent information on Kardex ■ Bibliography cards	■ Evaluation of care plans by instructor ■ Evaluation of clinical knowledge given by preceptor ■ Bibliography cards evaluated by instructor
4. To gain understanding of equipment utilized in step-down CCU	■ Observe other staff and preceptor ■ Attend March EKG course ■ Nursing literature	■ To be able to operate and read instruments accurately in the unit and report any abnormal findings to staff and physicians	■ Pass EKG course ■ Verbal and written evaluation by preceptor and staff
5. To relate laboratory test values of the cardiac disorders to the patients and assess how the results relate to their disorders	■ Examine types of lab tests ordered on cardiac patients ■ Spend half a day in the laboratory at the hospital ■ Staff and physicians ■ Lab manual	■ Log entries ■ Relating lab values of abnormal range in report to other staff members and physicians ■ Incorporation of lab data into monthly care plans	■ Evaluation of lab data incorporated in care plans by preceptor and instructor

Objective	Activities/Resources	Evaluation
6. Increase knowledge of and skill in administration of cardiac drugs	■ Assess patient's symptoms and associate symptoms with lab results ■ Check medication Kardex for commonly used drugs ■ Drug cards ■ Observe preceptor in methods of drug administration ■ Nursing literature ■ Medication in-service ■ Act as medication nurse for entire shift ■ Develop checklist to be used in evaluation ■ Pharmacology text, PDR	■ Medication cards written on the most commonly used cardiac drugs ■ Preceptor observes while medications passed ■ Log entries ■ Annotated bibliography showing good sources of drug information	■ Rating of procedures for drug administration by preceptor and self several times throughout semester ■ Evaluation of being medication nurse by self and preceptor ■ Evaluation of log and annotated bibliography by instructor
7. To gain skill in starting IV's and monitoring infusions	■ Observe preceptor, staff, and physicians starting IV's ■ Attend IV therapy course ■ Nursing literature	■ Log entries of literature read and experiences with IV's ■ Charts appropriate information about IV infusions	■ Pass IV therapy test ■ Evaluation of IV skills by preceptor ■ Review of log by instructor
8. Increase verbal communication skills with peers, staff, patients, and families	■ Observe preceptor's communication skills with patients, staff, families ■ Attend communication skills in-service ■ Use of cardiac teaching program ■ Develop a rating scale to measure communication effectiveness	■ Log entries ■ Effectively communicates verbally in conferences, shift reports, and on a 1:1 with staff, patients, and families	■ Rating of communication skills by peers, preceptor, and self through use of rating scale ■ Instructor comments on log entries
9. To improve ability to provide teaching to client and family	■ Preceptor ■ Cardiac instruction book ■ Closed-circuit TV cardiac teaching program ■ Field trip to American Heart Association ■ Field trip to Riverside Cardiac Rehabilitation Program ■ Teach families and clients weekly	■ Log entries on field trips ■ Presentation on services of AHA in clinical conference ■ Tape recording of two teaching sessions	■ Preceptor evaluation of teaching efforts ■ Instructor evaluation of log entries ■ Instructor and class evaluation of AHA conference ■ Instructor evaluation of taped teaching efforts

Student _____

Preceptor _____

Instructor _____

References

Asteriadis, G. T. "Contractual Learning: A Viable Approach to Education in the Biological Sciences." *American Biology Teacher*, Nov. 1976, *38*, 481–482.

Chickerella, B. G., and Lutz, W. J. "Professional Nurturance: Preceptorships for Undergraduate Nursing Students." *American Journal of Nursing*, Jan. 1981, *81*, 107–109.

Delaney, C., and Schoolcraft, V. "Promoting Autonomy: Clinical Contracts." *Journal of Nursing Education*, Nov. 1977, *16*, 22–28.

Knowles, M. S. *Self-Directed Learning: A Guide for Learners and Teachers*. New York: Cambridge Book Company, 1975.

Rauen, K., and Waring, B. "The Teaching Contract." *Nursing Outlook*, Sept. 1972, *20*, 594–596.

■ SELECTION 4

Using Contracts for Special Projects in a Course on Aging at the East Tennessee State University College of Medicine

☐ This selection illustrates the use of contracts for special projects within a short course, "Adulthood and Aging," at the Quillen-Dishner College of Medicine at East Tennessee State University. The course is one of the units in the curriculum for first-year medical students. As part of the course, learners are asked to design a special project in which they will study in depth one content area in which they have a special interest. The contract is negotiated with, and the evidence of accomplishment is evaluated by, a faculty consultant who has special resources in that area of interest. It is not uncommon for instructors to announce at the beginning of a course that students who want a B grade have only to accomplish the objectives in the course syllabus, but those who want an A grade must contract for a special project that takes into account their unique strengths, interests, and life goals.

The three contracts reproduced here are examples of such projects and illustrate the wide range of interests that can be taken into account through this approach.

This selection was provided by Robert D. Fox, director of the Center for Geriatrics and Gerontology at the East Tennessee University College of Medicine.

Adulthood and Aging: A Self-Directed Short Course
Learning Contract

Title of learning project _____ Changes in the Self-Concept in Aging

Name _____ Social Security # _____ Faculty consultant _____ Robert Fox

Learning Objectives	Learning Resources and Strategies	Evidence of Accomplishment	Validation of Evidence
Learn the changes in the self-concept in aging.	Lecture: "Retirement and the Use of Leisure Time" (Sept. 8) Books: ■ *Modern Synopsis of Comprehensive Textbook of Psychiatry II* by Freedman, Kaplan, and Sadock ■ *Aging from Birth to Death*, ed. by M. W. Riley ■ *Aging Better* by E. V. Cowdry ■ *The Daily Needs and Interests of Old People* by Adeline M. Hoffman ■ *Clinical Geropsychiatry* by Adrian Verweerdt ■ *Aging and Behavior* by Jack Botwinick Periodicals: ■ *Gerontologist*, Feb. 1980, *20*(1), 96–98	Oral presentation to small group with a documented written handout: ■ Mike Reed ■ Jim Wojcik ■ Will Hobbs	Written evaluation of handout by the Director of the Appalachian Christian Village. Evaluation form given to small-group members with criteria: ■ Quality of presentation ■ Evidence of knowledge ■ Clarity of information ■ Practicality to physicians ■ Organization of material

Adulthood and Aging: A Self-Directed Short Course
Learning Contract

Title of learning project ___ The Possibility of Embryonic Tissue Implants in the Treatment of Degenerative Mental Disorders

Name ___ Social Security # ___ Faculty consultant ___ Leo M. Harvill

Learning Objectives	Learning Resources and Strategies	Evidence of Accomplishment	Validation of Evidence
For my project I will evaluate the current status of research on embryonic tissue implants to replace degenerating CNS cells. In addition, I hope to assess the possibility that this will become a plausible method of treating degenerative mental disorders.	I have already consulted with Dr. Baisden and have received several literature leads, including "Reconstruction of Brain Circuitrics by Neural Transplants," *Trends in Neurosciences*, 2 (1979), No. 12, 301–308 and "A Unifying Hypothesis for the Cause of Amyotrophic Lateral Sclerosis, Parkinsonism, and Alzheimer's Disease," *Annals of Neurology*, 10:499–505, 1981. To gain more knowledge I now intend to undertake a computer search of the literature using the key words *transplantation, neural tissue, embryonic tissue, neocortical tissue, septohippocampal system, and degenerative mental disorders.*	I will submit an essay to Drs. Baisden and Woodruff reporting my findings and stating my conclusions.	Drs. Baisden and Woodruff will judge the quality of my investigation based on the content, clarity, accuracy, and usefulness of my essay as a guide to the research in this area. Afterward, they will submit a letter to Dr. Harvill confirming that I have met the above criteria.

Adulthood and Aging: A Self-Directed Short Course
Learning Contract

Title of learning project __Alternatives to Nursing Home Care for the Elderly__

Name _____ Social Security # _____ Faculty consultant _____ Ms. D. Dobbins

Satisfactory completion of contract will result in the award of Pass.

Learning Objectives (What will I know or be able to do after project is complete?)	Learning Resources and Strategies (What human and material resources will I use, and how will my actions be organized?)	Evidence of Accomplishment of Objectives (How will I demonstrate that I have reached my objectives?)	Validation of Evidence (Who will judge the quality of the evidence and on what basis?)
To identify this community's resources (programs and facilities in the Johnson City area) devoted to returning elderly patients to their daily lives.	My strategy will be to visit and interview administrators of the following JC area programs or organizations: Project ACCESS Home Aide Services to Elderly First TN Human Res. Agency (Nutrition Program) Volunteer Medical Rentals, Inc. Washington County AARP JC Senior Citizens Center The object of the interviews, each of which will be less than 1 hour in length, will be to determine the nature and cost of the supportive services offered the elderly by that organization. Emphasis will be placed on those services which might obviate the necessity of removing a person from his or her normal environment to be placed in a nursing home.	A brief (10–15 minute) oral report will be presented to my evaluators. It will consist of a summary of my findings with, where applicable, a comparison of the nature and costs of similar services offered by different organizations.	I ask that Ms. D. Dobbins and Dr. Bob Fox judge whether the information provided represents a basic outline, which might be of use to a new physician in the community, of the range and cost of services available to the elderly in the JC area.

Observations and Reflections

This chapter is concerned basically with the question of how to introduce change into a system or organization. As I see it, three strategies for introducing change are available to us.

One strategy is change by edict. Many successful changes have been made using this strategy—the desegregation of the military services, for example. But this strategy is available to us only if we have the authority to enforce the edict—which eliminates many of us. And even if we have that authority, the change cannot be successfully implemented unless those who are going to have to implement it are adequately prepared. In a way, the introduction of contract learning in the Capital University nursing program was by edict by the faculty. But note how carefully the faculty members prepared themselves and the learners for introducing the change.

A second strategy is change by persuasion. Many successful changes have been made using this strategy, too—the achievements of the labor movement, civil rights movement, and women's movement, for example. But this strategy is available to us only if (1) we are in a position in which people will listen to us and (2) we are persuasive. This eliminates some of the rest of us. The introduction of contract learning at the University of North Dakota Department of Social Work began as a result of persuasion and then moved quickly to the issuance of a faculty edict. When that did not work, the faculty moved to the third strategy.

The third strategy is change by piloting (or demonstration) and osmosis. This strategy is available to all of us to some extent. For example, when I started the graduate program in adult education at Boston University in 1960 (my first full-time teaching position), I entered the university system with all sorts of preconceptions about what the university would not permit me to do. During my first year, accordingly, I was a very controlling and didactic teacher. And I was miserable, because I was violating so many of the principles of adult learning that I had been promulgating in my writings. In the second year I decided to start experimenting to find out what I could get away with—and, lo and behold, I found that the university paid no attention to what was happening in my classroom, so long as the computer got grades and so long as I did not tamper with university policies or try to change other professors.

So I experimented with self-grading (which did not work, because some of my students were nuns who gave themselves C's and D's—nuns are supposed to be humble—and then turned in the most outstanding work), learning/teaching teams, learning contracts for one or two units of courses and special projects. My learners became so enthusiastic about their being released to learn that they started spreading the word to other students and faculty members. I remember getting a call in my third year there from a professor of educational philosophy who said, "Malcolm, I have five of your students in my Ed. Ph. 501 course who want to do contracts with me. What the dickens are they talking about?" I suggested that we have lunch together and I would explain what I was doing. He thought it made sense—"That means that the students will do more work and I'll have to do less." He experimented with those five and found that it worked so well that he adopted contract learning in all his courses the next year. This experience was repeated a number of times over the next few years; the students were the "persuaders," not I. This is what I mean by "osmosis." When I moved to North Carolina State University in 1974, I experimented with speeding up the process of osmosis by inviting faculty colleagues to observe sessions of my class occasionally to observe and evaluate what I was doing. I found that they became convinced of its worth and confident about doing it much more quickly than had happened at Boston University.

This is the strategy that was used at East Tennessee State University from the outset and eventually at the University of North Dakota.

FOUR

Independent Study

■ Contract learning is probably used more widely in independent study than in any other aspect of education. This is understandable, because learners in independent study often do not have the structure of a course syllabus and seldom have continuous access to an instructor for guidance. The inquiry structure and process guidance are built into a learning contract at the time of its negotiation, and usually both can be modified through renegotiation as the learner works at carrying out the contract.

This chapter presents four case descriptions of how contract learning is used in independent study. All are in institutions of higher education and all are for credit toward a degree.

The first selection, from the "Alternative Learning Experiences" program of Whatcom Community College, in Bellingham, Washington, describes how learners are linked with mentors through a "broker" to meet certain degree requirements through learning contracts. It includes excerpts from a "Handbook for Contract Learning" that guides the learners through the contracting process and an example of a contract for credit in a course in child development, which other students are taking by attending class on campus. Typically, younger learners fresh from high school graduation choose the class option, and older learners who are returning to college after some years away from academe choose the independent study option.

The second selection, from Empire State College, in New York, describes how learning contracts are used to assess credit earned through a variety of means. Empire State offers no courses; it awards degrees exclusively through assessment of learning. Its policy statement expresses the commitment of the college to fostering self-directed learning through involving the learners in planning and carrying out their own learning. An example of a contract for eight upper-division liberal arts credits for a study of women in American literature is included.

The third selection, from the East Central College Consortium, in Ohio, describes the process by which learners may take regular campus-based courses at any of the member colleges or may contract with the consortium for courses accomplished through independent study. In this latter case, a contract is negotiated with three parties: the instructor, a campus coordinator, and the consortium director. This selection includes brief excerpts from A Study Guide for Personal Education Planning, provided to the students, and an example of a contract for the course "Science and Literature."

The fourth selection, from Sinclair College Without Walls, in Dayton, Ohio, explains how learners contract with a core faculty member to achieve prescribed competencies in a course; the core faculty member then negotiates the acceptance of the contract with the faculty mentor who teaches the course. An example of a contract for a course in labor relations is included.

The contract forms used by these four institutions are different in format, but they contain the common elements of specifying learning objectives, learning resources and strategies, and evaluation of learning outcomes.

■SELECTION 5

Whatcom Community College: Independent Study Credit in Child Development

☐ One of the pioneer innovators in higher education, Whatcom Community College, in Bellingham, Washington, has developed an "Alternative Learning Experiences" program in which students are linked with mentors through a "broker" to meet certain degree requirements through learning contracts.

Learners are provided a "Handbook for Contract Learning," which guides them in clear language through the six-step contracting process used at the college. Excerpts from this handbook are reproduced here, followed by an example of a contract for credit in child development.

This information was provided by Judith Deiro, a member of the faculty and a broker at the college.

Of special interest:

☐ Helpful suggestions about how to write learning objectives (vague versus precise), in Step 1.

☐ A listing of various types of learning activities and how they should be specified, in Step 2.

☐ A listing of ways in which accomplishment of the objectives can be demonstrated and guidelines for developing criteria that demonstrate quality of learning for purposes of grading, in Step 3.

☐ Use of a learning resource center for identification of learning resources, in Step 4.

☐ Guidelines for estimating the amount of credit to be awarded based on the number of hours spent in learning a subject, in Step 5.

☐ Suggestions for how to use a mentor in negotiating a contract, in Step 6.

☐ Answers to questions frequently asked by learners about contract learning.

☐ Guidelines for self-evaluation of learning and of the contract learning process.

Handbook for Contract Learning

Introduction

Whatcom Community College offers you an exciting alternative approach to the traditional methods of learning in a college setting. You are encouraged to pursue learning outside the classroom through the guidance of a self-designed *learning contract.* A learning contract, though not a binding document in the strictly legal sense of *contract,* is a written agreement reached between the student and the college regarding what is going to be learned, the method of learning, and the method of evaluation. Contracts are drawn up, agreed to, and signed by you, your mentor, and the Coordinator for Alternative Learning, thus the name *learning contract.* A learning contract enables you to develop a course(s) specifically related to your own academic, career, and life interests.

How to Develop a Learning Contract

Step 1: Specify Your Learning Objectives

You and your mentor together agree on what the learning contract contains, but you have a major role in developing the contract. A mentor is an individual with expertise in the subject area of your learning experience recruited by the college to assist you through your learning contract.

Now you are ready to start filling out the first section of the learning contract, "Learning Objectives." A learning objective is a clear and concise statement that defines specifically what you want to learn. Learning objectives describe what you will learn, in whatever terms are most meaningful to you, and not *how* you are going to learn the material or subject. Here is an example of both vague statements and precise learning objectives in a course in Child Development:

Learning Objectives

    1. *Vague:*   Be able to understand the development of children.

      Precise: Be able to identify the process of physical development from birth to twelve years of age.

  2. *Vague:*   Be able to learn how a child thinks.
      Precise: Be able to compare and contrast theories for the learning process of a three- to five-year-old child.

You can write as many learning objectives as you want, within the scope of the learning experience.

Step 2: Specify Your Learning Activities

When you have finished listing your learning objectives, move to the second section of the contract, "Learning Activities." Learning activities describe how you propose to go about accomplishing *each* of the learning objectives. Identify the activities or strategies you will use to acquire the learning and the resources, material and human, you plan to use. Some examples of possible learning activities are:

1. *Travel*—Describe where you plan to travel and the length of time.
2. *Reading*—Include complete bibliography in appropriate section.
3. *Observations*—Describe what you expect to observe.
4. *Mentor consultation*—Indicate the approximate number of meetings, the time involved, and purpose.
5. *Working*—Describe your job duties and place of work.
6. *Community involvement/volunteer work*—Describe your expected volunteer activities and the approximate amount of time involved.
7. *Field trips*—Identify the location of the field trip.
8. *Journal*—Describe what you expect to be recording in the journal.
9. *Interviewing*—Identify the positions or persons.
10. *Workshops/training sessions*—Identify the workshop and the number of hours involved.
11. *Practice*—Specify number of hours per week.

Step 3: Specify How You Are Going to Demonstrate Learning

You now determine the method(s) of *evaluation*. An evaluation supplies evidence to the mentor that you have learned what you set out to learn and provides a basis for grading. You will want to discuss this with your mentor, but try to design a method of evaluation that is interesting, creative, and challenging to you. Be sure there is a method of evaluation for each learning objective. Some ideas for possible forms of evaluations that can be used are:

1. *Written research paper*—Identify topic, format, special expectations.
2. *Demonstration or simulation*—Role-play learning.
3. *Learning journal*—Describe what you expect to be recording in the journal.
4. *Oral evaluation*—Identify topics and format.
5. *Case study*—Identify subject and situation.
6. *Examination*—Objective or essay, in-class or take-home.
7. *Product assessment*—Specify product, for example, poems, paintings, photographs.
8. *Self-evaluation*—Follow the "Self-Evaluation Guidelines."
9. *Project or experiment*—Specify nature of the project or experiment.
10. *Performance*—Specify performance, for example, ballet, voice, skiing, and circumstances surrounding performance.
11. *Study questions*—Specify which readings or chapters covered.

Ideally evaluations take place periodically throughout the learning experience, allowing for opportunity to modify the learning contract or provide needed assistance.

A good suggestion or "rule of thumb" is to include a *learning journal* as one of your forms of evaluation. A learning journal is an informal, running record you keep of your discussions, activities, and reflections pertaining to the learning experience. Your learning journal will help you and your mentor target areas in which you are having difficulty, for example, management of time, organization, and progress of learning. It can also help you integrate the knowledge by reflecting on the learning experience.

In addition to method of evaluation, you need to specify the *criteria*. Criteria are the basis upon which the results of the evaluation methods are to be graded. You can do a learning contract for either a pass-fail grade or a letter grade. Most learning contracts are done on a pass-fail basis.

If you want to receive a letter grade, specific criteria must be set up indicating the level of accomplishment or expertise to be achieved for each grade level (A, B, C, D, and Z). You can determine the grade level by varying either the quantity of evidence (amount of work) you agree to supply *or* the quality of learning demonstrated in the evidence. A suggested guideline upon which to develop criteria demonstrating quality of learning is below.

Criteria for Demonstrating Quality of Learning

D   Marginal completion of learning activities with evidence of incomplete understanding of desired knowledge and/or skills demonstrated.

C   Completion of all learning activities with evidence of a basic understanding of desired knowledge and/or skills demonstrated.

B   Completion of all learning activities with *mastery* of the desired knowledge and/or skills demonstrated.

A   Completion of all learning activities with *mastery* of the subject *and* ability to demonstrate understanding of the general theory underlying subject and transfer this under-standing to applied/other situations.

Step 4: Supply Your Bibliography

If you know of the books or articles you want to read or filmstrips/slides and other materials you need in order to learn what you set out to learn, list them in the designated section. If you are unsure of some good reading resources or other material resources, you may want to check with the Learning Resource Center (LRC) to get some ideas (it would be time-saving to make an appointment with an LRC staff member, or have your broker introduce you to a staff member). You can also ask your mentor to recommend resources for your bibliography.

Step 5: Propose the Amount of Credit

Learning contracts vary in the amount of credit they are worth according to the time spent with the experience and depth and quality of the learning. In order to determine credit, you need to add up the number of hours you will spend learning the subject. Look at your list of activities and "guesstimate" the amount of time you will spend in each activity over the duration of the learning experience. Total the number of "estimated" hours. With the *total* number of hours, use the following chart to estimate your credit:

1 credit	22–33 hours
2 credits	34–66 hours
3 credits	67–99 hours
4 credits	100–132 hours
5 credits	133–165 hours
6 credits	166–198 hours
7 credits	199–231 hours
8 credits	232–264 hours
9 credits	265–297 hours
10 credits	298–330 hours
11 credits	331–363 hours
12 credits	364–396 hours

The broker or mentor may modify your proposed amount of credit based on his or her professional judgment of the depth and quality of the learning.

Step 6: Negotiate Your Contract with Your Mentor and Get Approval Signatures

After you have completed your draft of your learning contract, you will want to review it with your mentor. At the bottom of each section there is a place for the mentor to make any negotiated additions, deletions, comments, or revisions. Here are some questions you might ask your mentor about the contract to get optimal benefit from his or her expertise:

1. Are the learning objectives clear, understandable, and realistic; do they describe what you propose to learn?
2. Can he or she think of other objectives you might consider?
3. Do the learning activities seem reasonable, appropriate, and effective tools with which to learn the desired knowledge?
4. Can he or she think of other activities you might consider?
5. Does the evidence seem relevant to the various objectives, and would it be a valid way to evaluate the experience?
6. Can he or she suggest other evidence you might consider?
7. Are the criteria upon which to judge the evidence fair, clear, and understandable?
8. Does he or she have recommendations for other criteria?

Questions About Contract Learning

1. *How many credits can I receive by learning contracts from Whatcom Community College?*

    The type of degree you are receiving from WCC limits the number of credits you can obtain through independent learning. Please check with your academic adviser to make sure that your learning contract fits within your degree plan.

2. *How many credits can I receive by learning contract per quarter?*

    You may receive up to a maximum of twelve credits per quarter, but remember you determine the length of time needed to satisfactorily complete the learning contract. Most contracts are designed to be completed in a quarter, but they can be designed for a longer or shorter period of time. You may be working on a maximum of twelve credits at any time.

3. *How do I prove I spent the designated time on the learning contract?*

    It is not important that you "prove" the time spent. It is important that you prove the designated learning has taken place, which happens through the evaluation process.

4. *Is there a limit to how much credit I can receive for the same learning experience?*

    The learning experience sets the limits, not WCC. You receive credit for the learning acquired, not the time involved. Repeating an experience with no *new* learning does not equate to more college credits.

5. *May I have two different contracts simultaneously?*

    Yes. You can work on as many different contracts at a time as you feel capable of handling successfully, up to the maximum of twelve credits per quarter.

6. *What if I don't want to complete a contract?*

    You will need to see your broker to work through details. You may get credit for what you have already learned, or it may be decided that it is best for you to drop the course.

7. *Do I have to finish my contract in a certain time period?*

    You may begin and finish a learning contract at any time during the year, *except* for students receiving financial aid or veterans' benefits. Those students must finish the contract during the quarter in which they have registered for it.

8. *What if I need more time to complete my contract than I originally planned? Is there a penalty for an extension?*

    There is no penalty for an extension. You are asked to estimate the amount of time it will take you to complete the contract at the beginning. If you need more time, an extension must be negotiated and agreed upon by your mentor, and a new time limit established.

9. *Is it possible to revise a contract midstream?*

    Revisions in the contract are to be negotiated with the mentor. Put changes in writing in the appropriate section of the learning contract. If changes entail a revision in the number of credits, course title, course department, or major scope of the learning contract, your broker should be notified.

10. *How is my mentor selected?*

    Your mentor is selected by your broker on the basis of his or her expertise in the subject area. You may make a suggestion of a possible mentor, but the final selection is by the college.

11. *How much time can I spend with my mentor?*

   Mentors are advised to spend no more than twelve hours working on the contract, including time for preparation and evaluation. You make arrangements to meet with your mentor according to both of your time schedules, within the maximum of twelve hours per learning contract.

12. *What can I expect from my mentor?*

   The roles and responsibilities of the mentor, as well as the student's, are spelled out in the appendix.

13. *Can I change mentors in the middle of a learning contract?*

   Yes. You need to discuss your reasons with your broker.

14. *Is my mentor paid?*

   In most instances, your mentor is paid by WCC for the maximum of twelve hours of work with you and the learning contract.

15. *Who evaluates my learning . . . the college . . . my mentor?*

   The mentor is responsible for evaluating your learning. Any evidence you produce is for the mentor only. It is not to be submitted to the broker or WCC.

16. *Can I do a learning contract for a course regularly offered by the college?*

   Yes, if the subject can be learned on an independent basis.

17. *How are the department and course number determined?*

   Your broker, as an "educational officer," is responsible for determining department and course number (if the course is not a regular course offering at WCC). Course numbers will be 89, 99, 189, 199, 289, or 299, depending on the level of advancement of the study. Your mentor may make some suggestion in this area. Otherwise, regular WCC department and course numbers are used.

18. *How do I register for a learning contract?*

   You first contact a college broker to discuss the possibility of doing a learning contract, *prior* to registering. Number of credits will be determined, and you will then register for LC (learning contract) 189 for a predetermined number of credits.

19.   *Are independent learning credits transferable to other colleges? Do they satisfy degree requirements?*

Credits are transferable and can satisfy degree requirements, depending upon the learning contract and how the experience fits within your degree plan. Please contact your academic adviser if this is a concern to you.

20.   *If I am receiving veterans' benefits, are there any credit restrictions I should be aware of?*

If you are receiving veterans' benefits, you may earn credit through a learning contract, as long as it constitutes less than 50 percent of your quarter credit load. You must complete the contract during the quarter in which you have registered for it.

21.   *Can I do a learning contract outside of Whatcom County?*

Yes. If you are going to work or travel outside the county, you may design the experience into a learning contract.

22.   *What if I want to change a pass-fail to a letter grade?*

A change from pass-fail to a letter grade must be negotiated with your mentor, and definite criteria developed. If you want to change the grading scheme from a letter grade to pass-fail, you need to negotiate this also with your mentor.

Self-Evaluation Guidelines

The only person who really knows how much you have learned through your learning contract is *you*. Writing a self-evaluation provides you the opportunity to reflect on the academic and personal growth that has occurred as a result of your involvement with your learning contract. When composing the self-evaluation, you might think about the following questions, but feel free to respond in any way that provides a well thought out and sincere evaluation of your learning contract experience.

1.   Did I learn what I originally thought I was going to learn? What objectives were met and which were not?

2. What were some of the unanticipated learnings?
3. Why was I not able to achieve some of my expected goals?
4. What have I learned about myself as a result of being involved with the learning contract experience?
5. What have I learned about my ability to learn independently through a learning contract?
6. What new subject areas do I want to explore as a result of this learning experience?
7. What factors do I consider contributed to this learning experience being worthwhile (or not worthwhile)?
8. If I were going to do another learning contract, what would I do differently to maximize the value of the learning experience?

Sample Learning Contract

WHATCOM COMMUNITY COLLEGE
5217 Northwest Road
Bellingham, WA 98226
(206) 676-2170 / 384-1541

Learning Contract

Personal Information

Student Name
Address   *Zip*
Social Security Number
Day Telephone   *Evening Telephone*

Project Information

Course Title   Child Development
Department/Number   Psychology 210   *Number of Credits*   5
Pass/Fail   *Letter Grade*   XX   *Quarter*
Beginning Date   Sept. 22   *Estimated Completion Date*   Dec. 12
Mentor   Drew Oakley   *Telephone*   676-2109
Address   Midtown Center—WCC

Project Goal

> I would like to have a better knowledge of child develop-
> ment so I can better understand my children. Also, I would
> eventually like to teach and feel I would be a more effective
> teacher with a background in the process of the developing
> child.

For Official Use

Item #   *Grade*
Broker   Judith Deiro

1. *Learning Objectives*

What do you what to learn?
What knowledge, understanding, skill, attitude, or value is
    sought?
What questions do you have about your chosen topic?

1. Be able to identify the process of physical development
    from birth to twelve years of age.
2. Be able to compare and contrast theories for the
    learning process of a three- to five-year-old child.
3. Be able to describe how children develop sex roles and
    associated behavior.
4. Be able to describe how children's personalities develop
    according to different theories and learn how to help
    my child have a positive self-concept.
5. Be able to learn how to effectively discipline a child.
6. Be able to become more conscious of my role as a parent
    and how I can help my child develop to her fullest
    potential.

Mentor Comments/Negotiated Revisions

Are the objectives stated as clearly and specifically as
    possible?
To the best of your knowledge, are they equivalent to college-
    level learning?

Good objectives.

2. *Learning Activities*

How do you propose to acquire this learning?
What tasks, projects, experiences, exercises will you do?
Who are the people you will consult?
What places and resources will you utilize?

1. a. Read selected readings.
   b. Confer with mentor once a week for ten weeks to
       discuss concepts. One-hour meeting per week.

2. Same as 1a and b.
3. a. Volunteer at WCC Day Care Center six hours per week to observe children's behavior.
    b. Observe own children's behavior.
4. Same as activities 1, 2, and 3.
5. Same as activities 1, 2, and 3.
6. Keep a learning journal reflecting on my behavior in relation to what I am learning in the readings.

Mentor Comments/Negotiated Revisions

Is each objective accounted for with sufficient resources and activities?
Has specific time been identified for student/mentor conferencing?
What changes do you recommend in the learning activities?

   None

3. Evaluation

What evidence will you show your mentor to determine your learning?
What criteria will be used to evaluate this evidence?
If a letter grade is desired, indicate what is to be accomplished for each grade.

1. a. Submit research paper on *The Developing Child*, including footnotes, to be evaluated by mentor.
       A Integrate knowledge from readings with own observations, reflections, and thoughts
       B Interface and organize knowledge from readings
       C Demonstrate understanding of knowledge from readings
       D Incomplete grasp of concepts
    b. Submit annotated bibliography to be reviewed by mentor for completeness and accuracy.

    A Completion of all the selected readings
    B Completion of 5 of selected readings, including *The Developing Child*
    C Completion of 3 of selected readings, including *The Developing Child*

2. Same as 1a and 1b.
3. a. Submit learning journal of observations and reflections to be reviewed by mentor for completeness. Not to be graded.
   b. Oral evaluation with mentor on observations, readings, reflections demonstrating understanding of learning objectives to be evaluated based on guidelines in the Student Handbook.
4. Same as 1a and 1b.
5. Same as 1a and 1b.
6. Same as 3a.

Mentor Comments/Negotiated Revisions

Is there a method of evaluation to demonstrate fulfillment of each learning objective?
Has consensus been reached regarding criteria for evaluation?
What changes do you recommend regarding evaluation?

Journal will be checked at regular conference sessions.

4. ***Bibliography***

Please supply the proposed bibliography that will be used, including books, audiotapes, films. Submit additional page if necessary.

1. *The Developing Child*—Bee
2. *Total Baby Development*—Koch
3. *The First Three Years of Life*—White
4. *The Discovery of the Child*—Montessori
5. *Ourselves and Our Children*—Boston Women's Health Collective

6. *What Are Little Girls Made Of?*
7. Use LRC for magazine resources and media resources

5. *Contract Learning Student Check-Off List*

*Learning Contract
Development Process*   *Learning Process*

____ Contact College Broker   ____ Negotiate Revisions if
____ Design Learning   Necessary
Contract   ____ Complete Learning
____ Contact Mentor and Ne-   Objectives
gotiate Contract   ____ Evaluate Learning with
____ Submit Contract to   Mentor
Broker for College   ____ Request Mentor to Sub-
Approval   mit Grade to College
____ Register for Course

6. *Approvals*

The signatures below indicate that these individuals have
read this contract and approve it as an appropriate
academic experience.

Student   *Date*
Mentor   Drew Oakley   *Date*   Sept. 9
Broker   *Date*
Assistant Dean for Instruction   *Date*

■ SELECTION 6
Empire State College: Contracting
for Liberal Arts Credit

☐ Empire State College was founded by the Board of Trustees of
the State University of New York and by its first chancellor,
Ernest L. Boyer, in 1971. It is headquartered in Saratoga Springs
but has learning centers located throughout the state. It awards
associate of arts, associate of science, bachelor of arts, and
bachelor of science degrees. Previous credit or credit equivalents
are taken into account in granting advanced standing. The
college does not offer courses itself but awards degrees through
a process of assessment of learning obtained in a variety of ways.

Learning can occur in any or all of six modes: (1) formal
courses offered by any kind of institution, not only colleges and
universities, (2) cooperative studies, in which several students
with similar interests work together collaboratively, (3) tutorials,
in which a mentor guides an individual student through a
particular area of knowledge or competence, (4) organized self-
instructional programs, such as correspondence courses, programmed learning, or educational television, (5) direct experience, which may be supervised or unsupervised but permits
self-examination and reflection by the student, and (6) independent study by reading, writing, travel, or other means. The
student begins a program at any time during the year by
developing a contract in consultation with a mentor at one of the
centers.

Students are provided with a document, "Policies, Procedures, and Letters of Understanding," which opens with this
rationale for the program: "Empire State College is committed to
the idea that effective learning derives from purposes and needs
that are important to the individual; that learning occurs in
varied ways and places; and that styles of learning may differ
significantly from person to person and from one setting to
another. The College actively fosters the participation of each
student in the planning and designing of his or her education
through the use of individualized degree programs and learning

contracts." The document then provides specific guidelines for developing a learning contract and having the learning outcomes it specifies evaluated by the student and a mentor.

The following example of a contract is for eight upper-division liberal arts credits for a study of women in American fiction.

Of special interest:

□ The thoughtful evaluation by the mentor, which assesses not only the substantive knowledge gained about women in American fiction but also the student's growth in academic skills.

Sample Learning Contract

Contract Information

Name Contract No. 5
Address Begins on 7/12/82
Phone (area & number): Home Work Ends on 9/4/82
Social Security No. Credit Expected 8
Mentor's Name Code Final Contract ☐
Center Status ☒ Full-time ☐ Half-time

Give description of: (A) **PURPOSES** of this study; (B) **LEARN-ING ACTIVITIES** to be undertaken and (C) methods and criteria for **EVALUATION.** Use the underlined as headings for the three sections of the Contract.

A. *Purpose*

Women in American Fiction (8 upper-division liberal arts credits)

B. *Learning Activities*

The student will read:

Nathaniel Hawthorne, *The Scarlet Letter*
Kate Chopin, *The Awakening*
Henry James, *Washington Square* or *Portrait of a Lady*
Flannery O'Connor, three or four short stories
Agnes Smedley, *Daughter of Earth*
Charlotte Perkins Gilman, *The Yellow Wallpaper*
Toni Morrison, *Tar Baby*
Tillie Olsen, *Tell Me a Riddle,* "As I Stand Here Ironing"
Mary Gordon, *Company of Women* or *Final Payments*
Maxine Hong Kingston, *Woman Warrior*
Susan Schaeffer, *Anya*
March McCarthy, *Memories of a Catholic Girlhood*
Robert and Jane Hallowell Coles, *Women of Crisis* (one volume)
Patricia Meyer Sparks, *The Female Imagination*

and two of the following:

Elizabeth Janeway, *Man's World, Woman's Place; Between Myth and Morning: Woman Awakening*

Adrienne Rich, *Of Woman Born*
Robin Lakoff, *Language and Woman's Place*
Michelle Zimbalist Rosaldo and Louise Lamphere, *Woman, Culture and Society*
Elizabeth Friar Williams, *Notes of a Feminist Therapist*

Signatures

Student	Date
Mentor	Date
Assoc. Dean	Date

The student is interested in exploring women's roles as authors present them. She will generate questions related to this focus, questions such as: What role choices are available to women in each work? What influences in the women's lives create their roles and their choices? How do women adapt to or rebel against their roles? In what ways are the answers to the foregoing questions related to the novels' central themes? By what literary means does the author create the reader's response to the women characters? In what ways do the nonliterary readings help illuminate the novels?

The student will use a journal to reflect on her answers to these questions and her sense of their relevance to contemporary women and to her personally. She will also explore such questions in short papers (2-5 pp.) on each work or group of works. In a final, long paper she will address the question that has interested her most, clearly discussing the question itself and analyzing several novels (with textual examples) in the light of her discussion.

C. *Evaluation*

The mentor and the student will evaluate the student's posing and exploration of questions about women's roles and their literary representations. She is expected to be able to explain some of the theories in the nonliterary readings and use them to analyze the literature, with some sense, also, of the literary techniques the works use to create their themes.

Sample Contract Evaluation

Name   Contract No.   5
Social Security No.   Status   ☒ Full-time   ☐ Half-time
Began on 7/12/82   Ended on 9/4/82
Mentor's Name   Center   Credit Earned   8

I. *Topic of Study*

Women in American Fiction

II. *Evaluation*

The student was interested in learning more about women's past
and present roles, about the presentation and realism of these roles
in literature, and about good writing. She read Nathaniel
Hawthorne, *The Scarlet Letter;* Kate Chopin, *The Awakening;*
Henry James, *Washington Square* and *Portrait of a Lady;*
Flannery O'Connor, three or four short stories; Agnes Smedley,
Daughter of Earth; Charlotte Perkins Gilman, *The Yellow
Wallpaper;* Toni Morrison, *Tar Baby;* Tillie Olsen, *Tell Me a
Riddle,* "As I Stand Here Ironing"; Mary Gordon, *Final Payments;*
Maxine Hong Kingston, *Woman Warrior;* Susan Schaeffer, *Anya;*
March McCarthy, *Memories of a Catholic Girlhood;* Robert and
Jane Hallowell Coles, *Women of Crisis* (one volume); Patricia
Meyer Sparks, *The Female Imagination;* and Elizabeth Janeway,
*Man's World, Woman's Place; Between Myth and Morning:
Woman Awakening.*

The student worked independently, excited by her growing
confidence and improvement in her own writing and in her
perceptions of literary and women's issues. Her sixteen short
papers on each of the books and her longer paper exploring
women's power and powerlessness show a lively, critical mind
responding warmly to the characters and their situations and to
the writers whose own lives she briefly researched. Her papers give
good grounds for her own evaluation of her work, in which she
stresses both academic and personal learning: "I can read more

critically [now]. I am aware of style as it pertains to theme and how it can help support the writer's point of view. . . . As a woman I found that this contract was like a shot in the arm. My awareness of women's roles has been greatly heightened. . . . I realized the importance of being independent and free to choose."

Her papers are increasingly sophisticated in their use of quotation and analysis. Instead of simply sketching plot and character development, as in early papers, she uses examples of plot, character, and, as she says, style, to explore the writers' concerns and to relate them to her own response as a thinking, feeling woman reader. In her final (12 pp.) paper on "Power and Women," she integrates a discussion of the treatment of power in the lives of men and women in six of the novels, using Janeway's insights into powerlessness and women's roles to assess common personal and social limitations of women in different times and social classes. She moves well from discussions of power and role in general and in literary themes to close analysis of such techniques as dialogue, style, and symbol in particular novels, to comparisons and personal applications. She has achieved her goals for this contract very successfully, earning eight upper-division credits.

Student	Date
Mentor	Date
Assoc. Dean	Date

■ SELECTION 7

East Central College Consortium: Contracting with Multiple Sponsors

☐ The East Central College Consortium is a network of seven private liberal arts colleges with headquarters at Mount Union College, in Alliance, Ohio. Students may take regular campus-based courses at any of the member colleges or may contract with the consortium to earn credit for courses accomplished through independent study.

The policies and procedures governing this process are described first, showing how the interests of multiple sponsors are taken into account, followed by an example of a contract for the course "Science and Literature."

This selection is excerpted from *A Study Guide for Personal Education Planning,* by Thomas R. Conrad, a member of the faculty of the consortium, which is distributed to learners on registration.

Of special interest:

□   The use of contracts with multiple sponsors (instructor, campus coordinator, consortium director).

Learning Contracts in the Consortium Program
Policies and Procedures

1.   Definition—A learning contract is a document which specifies a course of study that is agreed upon by the student, supervising instructor, faculty adviser, and the Consortium director, and which includes the following key elements:
    1.   A brief statement relating this particular learning contract to the student's long-range plans.
    2.   The topic of this course of study and the learning objectives which this specific contract is intended to achieve.

3. The specific learning activities, including books to be read, papers to be written, and the frequency of meetings with the instructor.

4. The number of weeks or months within which the requirements of the learning contract are to be met by the student, with stated beginning and ending dates.

5. The criteria and methods of evaluation of the work done under the learning contracts.

A learning contract is equivalent to one course unit, which in turn is equivalent to 5 quarter hours or 3.3 semester hours, although in approved instances learning contracts may be written for multiple units of credit. Learning contracts may be amended with the approval of the instructor and the Consortium director.

2. A learning contract must be filed with proper signatures for all courses undertaken in the Consortium Program, including lower-level courses using prepared curriculum materials developed by Consortium faculty.

3. Copies of all learning contracts will be retained by the student, the instructor who is supervising the particular contract, the campus Consortium coordinator, and the Consortium Director's Office.

4. Learning contracts will be undertaken according to the following sequence of steps:

Step One—*Registration for Contract Learning*

1. The student completes the short registration for contract learning form that is available from the office of the campus Consortium degree coordinator.

2. The student returns the completed registration form and payment of tuition, by check, money order, or credit card, to the Consortium Director's Office.

3. The student receives a copy of the registration form and a receipt for tuition payment.

Step Two—*Completing and Filing the Learning Contract*

1. Upon receiving the signed registration form from the Consortium Director's Office, the student proceeds to negotiate the learning contract, using the forms available

from the campus coordinator of the Consortium Program.

2. The completed learning contract form must be approved by the student, the instructor, and the campus coordinator of the Consortium Program.

3. The completed form for contract learning is submitted to the Consortium Director's Office for approval.

4. The Consortium director approves the contract, signs it, and returns copies to those referred to in 2 above.

5. Upon receiving the approved learning contract form, the student commences work toward completion of the terms of the learning contract.

6. When the conditions of the learning contract have been fulfilled to the satisfaction of the student and the supervising instructor, the instructor submits the evaluation report form to the Consortium Office, where it is recorded in the student's file and a copy is sent to the student and to the campus coordinator of the Consortium Program.

Sample Learning Contract

EAST CENTRAL COLLEGE CONSORTIUM

ECCC Director's Office
Mount Union College
Alliance, Ohio 44601
(216) 821-5320

CONSORTIUM DEGREE PROGRAM—CONTRACT LEARNING FORM

Student's name
Home address
Home phone number
Title of this contract   "Science and Literature"
Beginning date   4-1-77   Projected ending date   7-3-77
Instructor's name   Larisa Kane   College   Mount Union

Instructions: In the space below describe briefly the relationship of this contract to your educational goals; the learning objectives of this specific contract; the learning activities to be undertaken such as books to read, papers to write, museums to visit, and so on; the criteria and methods of evaluation of the work done under this contract.

My long-range goal is to obtain an ECCC degree and then attend graduate school to become a certified social worker. (I am presently a social case aide.) "Science and Literature" (1 course unit), although not directly related to my long-range goal, will help me discover to what degree men and nations can estimate cause and effect relationships and deduce the impact (past, present, and future) of forces in their lives. This course will not only help me expand my own philosophy of life but also enable me to help others cope with the gripping question of fate.

Through this learning contract, I hope to gain: an introduction to the concepts of chance and causality; the ability to identify, compare, and analyze various concepts of chance and causality; the opportunity to discuss these concepts with my instructor and fellow students; and the ability to evaluate the impact of causal and chance experience on society and myself.

I will read the study guide for the course along with the following suggested books: (1) Richard Olson, *Science as Metaphor,* (2) Dietrich Schroder, *Physics and Its Fifth Dimension: Society,* (3) Morris Kline, *Mathematics in Western Culture,* (4) William Jones, *The Rhetoric of Science,* (5) Robert March, *Physics for Poets,* (6) J. Bronowski, *The Ascent of Man,* (7) Stephen Mason, *A History of Science,* (8) Robert Pirsig, *Zen and the Art of Motorcycle Maintenance,* (9) J. Bronowski, *The Common Sense of Science,* (10) Walter Jackson Bate, ed., *Criticism: The Major Texts,* (11) Louis Bredvold et al., ed., *Eighteenth Century Poetry and Prose,* and (12) Robert Coover, *The Universal Baseball Association: J. Henry Waugh, Prop.* I will discuss each book with my instructor and, when possible, with other students in the course. I will meet with my instructor every week. As the culminating exercise of this contract, I will take slides of how I see chance and causality in my environment and prepare them for an audiovisual presentation.

My instructor will evaluate me on the basis of my discussions and on my slide presentation.

Signatures:

Student	Date
Instructor	Date
Campus Consortium Degree Coordinator	Date
Executive Director of the ECCC	Date

■ SELECTION 8

Sinclair College Without Walls:
A Course in Labor Relations

□ The College Without Walls was established in 1978 at Sinclair Community College, in Dayton, Ohio, as "an alternative to traditional higher education; it allows you to integrate your life and work experience into a self-directed associate degree program," as its brochure explains. The modal age group is thirty-one to thirty-five, many learners being older than that.

On admission the student meets with a core faculty member (of whom there are three, serving about 160 students in a variety of degree programs) to construct a first course contract. The contract has three sections: "Competencies," which are specified for each course, "Learning Activities," and "Evaluation." Students are asked to come to this meeting with some ideas about learning activities they would like to engage in. These ideas are discussed and sifted to help achieve a balance between experiential and theoretical learning. CWW students are required to read the same textbooks as the classroom students, but they are encouraged to include other strategies and resources, such as interviewing practitioners in the field, studying relevant problems on the job, designing field projects, and using the media programs in the Learning Resources Center. Special attention is given to "Evaluation," in which the student and core faculty member agree on what evidence will be produced to demonstrate the achievement of the competencies.

Once the contract is in good shape, the student and core faculty member sign it, and the core faculty member negotiates its acceptance with the faculty mentor who teaches the course, who signs it and takes over working with the student. Contracts can be changed, if circumstances warrant, by agreement among all three parties. The time frame for completion is flexible. Students are not tied to the quarter calendar: they can take up to another quarter to finish or can finish in two or three weeks. The student and core faculty member also agree on the formation of a Student Resource Group of five persons—the student, the adviser, a CWW peer, and two community resource persons. Most students use this resource group individually for psychic support and linkage with community resources.

The sample learning contract that follows is extracted from *A Student Guide to College Without Walls at Sinclair Community College*, published by the college. Included also is a "Summary of Learning and Documentation" form and an assessment form used as part of the evaluation process. The latter is especially useful in that it defines five competency levels.

This information was supplied by Gordon Cowperthwaite, professor and core faculty member, College Without Walls.

Of special interest:

☐ The central role of a core faculty member.
☐ The building into the contracting process of a support group.
☐ The specification of five competency levels.

Sample Learning Contract

SINCLAIR COLLEGE WITHOUT WALLS —LEARNING CONTRACT—

Student's Name   Address
Zip   Phone: Home   Work
Submission Date   1/7/84   Completion Date   4/14/84
Subject Area(s)   LAS 2ll

A.   Competencies: Please identify on page two all competencies related to the course(s) treated in this contract.

B.   Learning Activities: (How are you going to learn it—resources? strategies?)

☐ PROJECT   ☐ ESSAY/PAPER
☒ JOURNAL ARTICLES   ☐ ATTEND SELECTED
☐ A/V MATERIALS IN LRC   CLASS SESSIONS
☐ CASE STUDY OR   ☐ SPECIAL TUTORIAL W/
   SIMULATION   COMMUNITY
                                 PRACTITIONER
                             ☒ TEXT READINGS

OTHER   Interviews
NOTE: Please identify in detail on page two all learning activities to be completed for this contract.

C.   Evaluation: (How are you and your mentor going to know you learned it—evidence?) Please detail evaluation methods on page three.

☒ VERBAL DIALOGUE   ☐ PAPER & PENCIL TEST
☒ PRODUCT   (objective)
   EVALUATION   ☐ PAPER & PENCIL TEST
☐ CASE STUDY   (essay)
   EVALUATION   ☐ PERFORMANCE
                                EVALUATION

OTHER

Signatures   *Telephone*   *Office No.*   *Office Hrs.*   *Date*

Student
Core Faculty
Faculty Mentor
Faculty Mentor
Faculty Mentor

A. *Competencies*
  1. Understand labor and the management community.
  2. Identify the negotiation and administration process of the labor agreement.
  3. Discuss the historical and legal framework of organized labor.
  4. Define and discuss union behavior and the organizing table.
  5. Define and discuss grievance procedure, collective bargaining, wage and benefit issues.
  6. Identify cause and effect of labor unrest.
B. *Written description of learning activities* (How are you going to learn it—resources? strategies?)
  1. Utilize the book *Labor Relations* by Sloane and Whitney (which I have acquired) as a resource for this course.
  2. Interview Mr. Harold Barrett, Jr., assistant professor, Labor Studies, Sinclair Community College, regarding the current understanding of American union-management relations in regard to historical, legal frameworks and basic collective bargaining relationships.
  3. Interview Mr. John D. Beckham, retired civilian personnel officer, Defense Electronic Supply Center, regarding labor laws and regulations, cause and effect of labor unrest, negotiations, grievance procedures, labor-management cooperation, and trade unions.
  4. Research 6–8 articles on the following topics:
      Legal Framework
      Union Behavior
      Wage Issues

C. *Evaluation* (How are you and your mentor going to know
    you learned it—evidence?)
    1. Presentation of a 10–15-page paper interrelating view-
        points of practitioners with the principles learned in the
        textbook.
    2. Presentation of a 12–15-page paper detailing learning
        from the interview with Mr. Barrett.
    3. Presentation of an 8–10-page paper discussing the
        learning from the interview with Mr. Beckham.
    4. Presentation of a 3–5-page summary on the learning
        from *each* article researched.
    5. Dialogue with mentor.

Any special comments about your learning activities or evaluation
that your core and mentor need to know.

TO BE COMPLETED BY CORE FACULTY

Date Assessed   ——
Letter Grade   ——
Date: Change of Grade Submitted to Registrar's Office   ——
Grade Noted on Original Roster   ——

Sample Summary of Learning and Documentation
LABOR RELATIONS   LAS 211

Educational Experience	Description of Learning	Documentation
1. I utilized the book *Labor Relations*, by Sloane and Whitney, as a resource document for the preparation of an 11-page paper interrelating viewpoints of the practitioners with the principles I learned in the text.	I learned that labor relations is the interaction between two organizations— management and the labor union; and the parties to this interaction are always subject to various, often complex, environmental influences.	A
2. I interviewed Mr. Hal Barrett,assistant professor, and head of the Department of Labor Studies, Sinclair Community College. I then wrote a 13-page paper regarding the current understanding of American unions.	I learned the concepts of negotiation of and administration of labor agreements, with the emphasis on the development and application of the more significant bargaining issues, the interaction between two organizations—management and labor unions.	B
3. I interviewed Mr. John D. Beckham, retired civilian personnel officer, DESC, regarding negotiation and grievance procedures and labor-management cooperation. I wrote a 10-page paper on his concepts.	I discovered from this interview regarding management and the labor union that the parties to this interaction are always subject to various, often complex, environmental influences.	C

"Public Administration as Political Process" by John Rehfus, and "Collective Bargaining" by Beal, Wickersham, and Kienast.

From this research I learned from the economic viewpoint that bargaining parties commonly utilize three principles: comparative norm; ability to pay; and standard-of-living criteria for private industry bargaining. I also learned that a great deal more takes place in "contract language" on procedures, restraints, rights, and "shop rules." In the public sector—especially in federal—none of the three principles actually applies across the bargaining table.

D

Documentation A
   An 11-page paper interrelating viewpoints of the practitioners with principles learned from textbook.
Documentation B
   A 13-page paper detailing the learning from the interview with Mr. Barrett (a nationally known leader in the labor movement).
Documentation C
   A 10-page paper discussing the concepts learned from my interview with Mr. Beckham.
Documentation D
   Summaries of the following articles:
      "The Unions" by Martin Estey
      "Public Administration as Political Process" by John Rehfus
      "Collective Bargaining" by Beal, Wickersham, and Kienast

Assessment Form

SINCLAIR COMMUNITY COLLEGE

TO:

FROM: COLLEGE WITHOUT WALLS OFFICE (Room 6130)

DATE:

RE: ASSESSMENT FORM FOR CWW LEARNING
CONTRACT

1) Student's Name:
2) Telephone Number: (Work)   (Home)
3) Major:
4) Contracted Course:

It is my judgment that

(student's name)

1) has completed the Learning Contract for the course: _____
for _____ credit hours and should be awarded the following grade;

A, Competency level 1: the student knows, can apply, and values
the information/skill area at an excep-
tional level of competency

B, Competency level 2: the student has a good understanding of
this information/skill area and has had
the opportunity to apply it

C, Competency level 3: the student has an average understanding
and background in this information/skill
area

D, Competency level 4: the student has a limited understanding
and background in this information/skill
area

F, Competency level 5: the student has an unsatisfactory understanding and background in this infor-
mation skill area.

2)   has not adequately demonstrated competency and will need to
     provide the following additional work:

Basis of Assessment: _____
_____

Comments: _____
_____

_____ (Date for final assessment)_____
    Date   Faculty-Mentor Signature

Observations and Reflections

One of the keys to effective use of contract learning is obviously preparation of the learners for engaging in a strange new approach to learning. All four institutions included in this chapter provide the learners with a document that gives a rationale for this approach to learning and provides helpful step-by-step suggestions for drafting the contract. I find Whatcom Community College's "Handbook for Contract Learning" the clearest and most specific guide I have seen, and that is why I have reproduced extensive excerpts here.

Another preparatory strategy is a short workshop or seminar in which learners are informed about the process and engage in practice exercises designed to develop skill in formulating objectives, identifying resources and learning strategies, and specifying evidence for evaluating learning outcomes. Whatcom Community College uses this approach. In the three other institutions this responsibility is carried by the mentor, the core faculty member, or the campus coordinator and accomplished through individual counseling.

Another key to success is the provision of continuing support for the learners during the process of carrying out the contract. Sinclair College Without Walls provides a support group consisting of a peer, an adviser, and two community resource persons. The other institutions encourage the learners to use their mentors for continuing support and make specific suggestions about how to do so.

All four institutions provide that the contract can be renegotiated during the process and give specific instructions about the procedures to follow.

There is some variation in the degree of freedom the learners are allowed in specifying objectives. At Sinclair the competencies to be achieved in each course are specified by the institution, leaving the student to propose the resources and strategies for achieving them. In the other three institutions, learners are asked to take the initiative in proposing objectives, resources and strategies, and evaluation procedures, subject to agreement by the mentor through negotiation.

I was impressed by the emphasis in all four institutions on qualitative evaluation over quantitative measures. I found the mentor's evaluative comments in the sample contract from Empire State College an especially revealing example of this approach.

In a follow-up interview I asked Judith Deiro of Whatcom Community College whether contract learning seemed to be more appropriate for some learners and some subjects than for others. She reported that highly dependent and unmotivated learners did not do well with contract learning and were counseled into regular classroom courses. Learners fresh out of high school and the military service tended to predominate in this group. The only courses that do not seem to lend themselves to contract learning are those having to do with the development of interpersonal skills, in which group interaction is necessary.

⊞ FIVE ⊞

Academic Classrooms

■ *Learning contracts are being used increasingly in academic courses meeting in classrooms on campus as a way of involving the learners in taking some degree of responsibility for planning and carrying out their own learning and as a way to accommodate individual differences in background, learning needs and interests, learning styles, and the like. But campus-based instructors tend to feel more constrained by institutional traditions, policies, rules and regulations, and academic standards than do instructors in independent study programs. Therefore, the contracts presented in this chapter tend to involve more control by the instructors and less freedom for the learners to take the initiative. The selections demonstrate how some instructors are trying to provide a structural framework (for example, by prescribing objectives) that will appear to conform to institutional expectations while permitting varying degrees of learner initiative. The selections are arranged roughly in a sequence from greatest to least learner freedom.*

The first selection presents two contracts that were developed collaboratively by two learners in a graduate course, "Psychology of Adult Education," at the University of Nebraska. Each learner contracted for one objective common to both and two objectives that are somewhat different. Then both contracts provided for a collaborative project. The learners indicated what grade they wanted to receive, the instructor making the final judgment.

The second selection describes the procedures used in an undergraduate course, "Principles of Management," at Hillsdale College, in Michigan. The objectives of the course are prescribed by the instructor, but learners are given freedom to take the initiative in proposing how they will accomplish those objectives and how their efforts will be evaluated. But learners who wish to depart from this "standard format" may construct a completely individualized contract and negotiate it with the instructor. The instructor retains final responsibility for determining the grade.

The third selection presents two contracts in a graduate course, "The Adult Learner," at Virginia Commonwealth University. The instructor provides the learners with a set of required objectives for the course, but the learners can negotiate with her for modification of the objectives and inclusion of learning strategies other than the required readings. The two contracts illustrate the flexibility of the contract learning process in accommodating individual differences in pursuing common subject matter content. The final grade is determined by the instructor.

The fourth selection describes the procedures used in an undergraduate course, "Business Communications," at Brandon University, in Manitoba, Canada. The instructor prescribes the objectives, strategies, and evaluative evidence for a "base assignment," which yields a grade of C, and then provides a range of options for the learners to choose from in constructing contracts for a B or an A. The instructor retains final responsibility for determining the grade.

The fifth selection describes the policies and procedures used for a different kind of learner/instructor negotiation in a course, "The Development of the Young Child," at Augusta College, Augusta, Georgia. The instructor presents eight prescribed learning activities, and the learners are given some choices in how and at what depth they will be carried out. The learners then negotiate the percentage value that each activity will contribute to the final grade. Final decision on the grade rests with the instructor.

Another example of a graduate course in which the learners are given wide freedom in taking the initiative for constructing contracts is given in Chapter One.

■SELECTION 9

University of Nebraska: Collaborative Contracting in "Psychology of Adult Education"

☐ Students frequently ask their instructors whether they can contract to work in pairs or as a team. This selection consists of two contracts for a "Psychology of Adult Education" course in the graduate program in adult education at the University of Nebraska. Notice that the individual sections of the contracts have one objective in common—knowledge and understanding of learning theory—and two that are somewhat different. The joint project is included in the first contract.

   This selection was submitted by Mary Jane Evan, professor of adult education at the University of Nebraska.

Of special interest:

☐   Individualized contracts with one common and two different objectives for the same course.
☐   A collaborative project to apply the students' learnings to their work situation at the Boys Town Center for the Study of Youth Development.
☐   A request for the same grade (which was granted and achieved).

Course Contract
Psychology of Adult Education
Melinda J. Bickerstaff

Section I: Personal Learning Goals for the Course

Goals—Where am I going?	How shall I get there?	How will I know I've arrived?
1. To learn how I as an adult relate to others (mostly adults) in a wide variety of situations—as a supervisor, colleague, co-worker, instructor, and learner.	1. To use the materials and readings of this course, Neugarten, Perry, Adult Life Stages, Productivity, Motivation, and Work Cognitive Styles, to learn about adult psychology.	1. When I can write a description of several adults with whom I relate using the concepts of life stages, productivity, motivation, work, and cognitive styles.
	2. To compile this information and synthesize it for myself to determine and label my own cognitive style, most effective way of learning, and current life-style.	2. When this description can be used to more effectively clarify the relationship, expectations, and future goals for each of us.
	3. To talk with many adults of varying ages about how they view their current life stage, what they know about how they best learn, and so on.	
2. To learn more about learning theory, particularly as it relates to adults.	1. To begin with an overview of learning theories I've been exposed to in other graduate courses.	1. When I can write or verbally describe my own learning theory using the continuum of the Four Models of Man.
	2. To complete the course reading requirements and tasks concerning learning theory.	2. When my position contains sound research rationales.

3. To synthesize the knowledge and experience gained in this course with my current knowledge about leadership and how groups work and apply all this to my current work situation as the director of educational and training service programs for adults.

3. To focus my reading objectives on such authors as Bloom, *Taxonomy of Educational Objectives: Cognitive Domain*, and Krathwohl, *The Affective Domain*.

4. Because I work with other learning program planners on a daily basis, I will continually ask questions to ascertain their learning theories or models of man from which each plans. (This task will particularly apply when working with other trainers, as most learning program planners do not operate out of some learning theory framework.)

1. To develop fairly simple, yet informative, handouts for such concepts as Models of Man, cognitive styles, and program goals for the researchers with whom I work.

2. To develop an instrument that will assist the researchers in analyzing their program audiences in an informative, yet quick, manner.

3. To use these handouts with other learning program planners with whom I work.

4. To continually test out these handouts and materials to see if in fact they make a difference in the success or failure of the learning program.

3. When my position can be used to clearly explain the pros and cons of a program methodology or design I would use or recommend to other learning program planners.

1. When I can see that a feedback methodology or instrument that will let me know if this knowledge application has made a difference.

2. When I can pull together this synthesized knowledge and experience about the psychology of adults, leadership, and how groups work best into a written manual (with lots of visuals) for use with other learning program planners.

Section II: Final Course Project

The final project for this course will be a joint paper prepared by Melinda Bickerstaff and Marilyn Fischbach regarding our work situation. For the past two years we have been responsible for the creation and development of a Continuing Learning Center at the Boys Town Center for the Study of Youth Development. We are jointly responsible for providing learning settings and learning experiences for adults.

Following is an outline of our proposed project:

A. *Situation*

The Continuing Learning Center schedules twenty to thirty learning and educational programs for adults per month. The Learning Center staff works with program planners from a wide variety of disciplines and assists them in using the Learning Center to facilitate their programs.

What we would like to do is design and prepare materials that we could use with program planners in order to make them aware of some of the principles of adult learning and help them incorporate these principles into their program planning.

The physical environment of the Continuing Learning Center is conducive to adult learning. As directors of the center, we want to ensure that program content presented in our facility is also conducive to adult learning.

B. *The Process*

The initial task is to completely familiarize ourselves with the materials and readings in this course. Our goal is to become knowledgeable about the works, theories, and concepts of at least five to seven professionals currently doing research in the area of adult education.

The second task is to design instruments or methods that will assist program planners in analyzing the kinds of audiences for whom their courses, conferences, seminars, and programs will be aimed. Several adult learning theories such as Neugarten's life stages, cognitive styles, and right and left brain hemispheres will be used as the basis for the development of these analysis instruments.

The final stage of this process is to demonstrate the synthesis of our learning about adult psychology in this course by developing "hands-on" materials to be used by program planners that will help them to incorporate some of the principles of adult learning into their program designs.

C. *Products*

1. We will jointly prepare a ten- to fifteen-page summary of adult education principles. We will briefly deal with the psychology of adults and adult learning concepts and theory. We will not attempt to present a comprehensive review of all theories or concepts, but rather highlight several. Our writing style will be informal rather than academic, and we will make use of anecdotes to explain theory.

2. We will jointly prepare a comprehensive bibliography about adult education that can be used by program planners.

3. Each of us will analyze the learning needs of two adult groups who will potentially use the Continuing Learning Center for working conferences. (One audience will be local practitioners who work with abused adolescents, and the second group will be graduate school faculty who teach courses in public policy.) To facilitate the analysis, we will develop assessment tools related to learning theory.

4. We will submit a rough draft of a manual to be used by and with program planners who use the facilities of the Continuing Learning Center. This manual will demon-

strate how the principles of adult learning can be incorporated into practical application.

D. *Grades*

For our joint and individual efforts in working on this project, we are each seeking an A grade on the project.

Section III: Final Exam

I wish to take a take-home written exam and want to earn an A grade.

Section IV: Assistance from Instructor

I would like to make an appointment with the instructor at her office in Lincoln and spend an hour (or lunch) specifically talking about adult education and its application.

Course Contract
Psychology of Adult Education
Marilyn Fischbach

Goals—Where am I going?	How shall I get there?	How will I know I've arrived?
1. Become familiar with current literature in the field of adult education.	▪ Read the material listed in the course syllabus, keeping biographical notes on all authors. ▪ Talk with the reference librarian at the Boys Town Center Library to develop a list of journals dealing with adult education and psychology. ▪ Review back issues of journals, noting the editorial boards, contributing authors, and overall themes. ▪ Talk with instructor for recommendations of what are the new and upcoming areas of research in the field of adult education.	▪ When I can name five to seven professionals currently writing and doing research in the area of adult education. ▪ I want to be able to identify the institution or corporation they are with and the area they are currently writing or researching. ▪ When I can name the major research areas in adult education, where the research is being done, and by whom.
2. Become familiar with learning theory and how it pertains to adults.	▪ Read the course material in Area III and participate in class projects in order to develop an overview of learning theory. ▪ Review notes from past psychology and education courses that pertain to learning theory. ▪ Observe programs that are being held at the Continuing Learning Center and attempt to note what philosophy of man is providing the basis for instruction and what learning theories are being employed.	▪ When I can write my own approach to learning theory with appropriate rationales and show how my approach relates to current theory. ▪ When I can sit in on a workshop or conference and identify the learning theory being employed.
3. Relate my day-to-day work situation as a director of a learning center to the principles of adult education.	▪ Review reading material from the course and find common elements that fit my philosophy of man and my approach to adult psychology. ▪ Analyze my current job responsibilities and identify situations when I am responsible for the direct or indirect teaching of adults and begin to analyze the teaching situations in order to be able to identify cognitive styles, hemispheric preferences, developmental stages, and self-concepts. ▪ Begin work on my final project in which I will create planning tools that I can use with program designers.	▪ When I can identify a specific job responsibility and relate it directly to relevant aspects of the psychology of adult education. ▪ When I have completed the final project for this course.

■SELECTION 10

Hillsdale College: Undergraduate Course in "Principles of Management"

☐ For several years Hillsdale College, Hillsdale, Michigan, has offered an undergraduate program in business management sponsored jointly with the Dana Corporation, Toledo, Ohio. The program consists of three semester-long campus-based courses and four intensive "Dana Enrichment Seminars" conducted in a conference center between semesters. The program is based on the andragogical model.

The sample contracts presented here are for a campus course, Business 400, "Principles of Management: Theory and Practice," for three credits. The contracting process involves three thirty-minute sessions between each learner and the course facilitator: (1) at the beginning of the semester to negotiate the contract, (2) at the middle of the semester to monitor progress, and (3) at the end of the semester for the learners to present their evidence of accomplishment of the objectives. The course syllabus prescribes nine objectives (although the learners have the initiative to propose how the objectives will be accomplished), and the learners specify four additional personal objectives.

At the end of each semester, the facilitator chooses four learners to serve as Learning Team Leaders (LTLs)—in effect, teaching assistants—for four to six beginning learners the following semester, thereby giving them an opportunity to sharpen their skills of group leadership.

The first contract is in the standard format, specifying the nine prescribed objectives. Note, however, that the learner specifies what resources and strategies will be used to accomplish each objective, what evidence of accomplishment will be collected, and how that evidence will be validated. The second contract is an example of a learner's taking the initiative to depart from the standard format and constructing a highly individualized contract (jointly with another learner), subject to the facilitator's approval.

This selection was submitted by R. T. Williams, Dana Professor of Enterprise Management at Hillsdale College.

Of special interest:

□ A contract in which the objectives are set by the instructor but the learner takes the initiative in proposing resources and strategies for accomplishing them.

□ A totally learner-initiated individualized contract (jointly with another learner).

□ The process by which contracts are negotiated, monitored, and evaluated.

Sample Learning Contract

Participant __Jeff__ LTL (#2) Mike A.   Course __400A__   Semester __Spring 1985__   Date Started __1/85__   Date Completed __4/85__

	What I Am Going to Learn (Objectives)	How I Am Going to Learn It (Resources & Strategies)	Target Date for Completion (Time Frame)	How I Am Going to Know That I Have Learned It (Evidence)	How I Am Going to Document/Prove I Have Learned It (Verification by LTL, Learning Team Member, or Other)
1.	Increase my skills in relating to an authority figure as a resource for my learning.	Todd Slater	4/85	Voting & motions	Verified by Todd Slater
2.	Improve my skills in being able to teach and learn from my peers.	Management class	4/85	Evaluations & feedback scores	Evaluations & feedback scores
3.	Improve my skills in being able to relate to my peers as collaborators and more than competitors.	Getting motion passed in Federation	3/85	The motion being passed	Passed unanimously
4.	Increase my skills as a self-directed learner in addition to my skills as a teacher-directed learner.	Learned the aerobics workout	3/85	Being appointed captain	Was appointed captain
5.	Apply what I already know and can learn to more effectively manage my time and to have better control of my life.	Desk calendar	3/85	No missed appointments, having spare time	Calendar itself
6.	Identify and strengthen my greatest skill as a leader/influencer of others.	Being a supporter to Federation president	3/85	Motion getting passed	Verified by Cleves Delp
7.	Identify and develop the skill where I need the most growth as a leader/influencer of others.	Speaking in public	4/85	Class evaluation	Comments on evaluation were good
8.	Identify and develop the leadership/management knowledge, skill, and understanding that will give me a greater sense of life purpose and direction.	Being field house manager	4/85	Applying listening skill as manager	Better work from Janet
9.	Identify and develop the skills that will enable me to view change as a challenge more than as a threat.	Weekend meetings	4/85	By going to the meetings and enjoying them	I liked them

Upon Completion:

		April 15, 1985
Participant		Date
		A
Facilitator		Final Grade

1. I used the President of Men's Council as my resource. My strategy was to learn the correct way for interpreting the rules and regulations and applying them to violations. Completed 4/85. My application and interpretation of the rules and regulations, as learned from Todd Slater, are evidenced by my voting and motions made in Men's Council meetings.

2. I used my management class as my resource. My strategy was to be effective in my presentations and to do well on feedbacks due to my peers' presentations. Completed 4/85. My evidence for being an effective presenter is my evaluation sheets (majority felt they learned quite a lot), and my 89 percent average on my feedbacks was helped by my peers' presentations.

3. I used my position as Independent Federation Representative for my resource. My strategy was to convince and work together with other members of Federation to get a motion for including officer salaries into the by-laws so as to take the decision load off Finance Board. Completed 3/85. As evidence of the collaboration, the motion will be discussed and passed at next week's meeting.

4. I used my football aerobics workouts as my resource. My strategy was to not only be able to do the exercises but to do them well. This would be helped by daily stretching before the workout and extra time on the exercises. Completed 3/85. My evidence included my appointment as an aerobics leader due to the ability to do the workouts well.

5. I used a large desk calendar for my resource. My strategy was to get my work done on a regular basis and not forget appointments. Completed 3/85. My ability to make appointments and make them on time in addition to having spare time due to organization will be my evidence.

6. I used Cleves Delp, the president of Federation, as my resource. My strategy was to be supportive of an idea of Cleves's and influencing other members of Federation to agree to his idea. Completed 3/85. The motion to have extended hours in the Union and Ethan Allen Room for study and social purposes being passed is evidence of myself being supportive.

7. I used Management 400A as my resource. My strategy was to be a better public speaker and to develop this through class presentations. Completed 4/85. The comments and high ratings on my evaluation sheets provide the evidence that my public speaking skill is being developed.

8. I used my job as field house manager as my resource. My strategy was to apply listening to my boss/subordinate relationship. Completed 4/85. The evidence of this application could be seen in the efficiency and good work of employees. This is seen by my listening and understanding of Janet missing a day of work due to a severe sickness. She now is one of the better workers.

9. I used the meetings and seminars for Management 400A as my resource. My strategy was to view the weekend seminars and meetings as a chance to learn rather than a threat to my weekend plans. Completed 4/85. My great interest in Larry Lottier and his fabulous teaching ability is the evidence for viewing change as a challenge rather than a threat. I very much enjoyed the seminar and actually did not feel bad about sacrificing my weekend.

Memorandum

DATE: 4-13-85
TO: R.   R. T. Williams
FROM:
SUBJECT: Learning Contract: An Andragogical Approach

Instead of using the standardized learning contract provided by Professor R. T. Williams, Sara Dumke and I took it upon ourselves to develop a learning contract. I originally was going to use the established learning contract, but in order to better facilitate my learnings, Sara and I developed our own. We believe that it ran in conjunction with the spirit of the class—andragogy.

Using the learning resource guide, we developed our own learning contract. Our learning contract contains the following areas:

Self-evaluation
Listening
Motivation
Group decision and problem solving
Changes in ourselves as evidenced by each other

Our goal is to develop a contract that takes all areas of the class and combines them into one comprehensive unit.

Self-Evaluation: Before any learning could be accomplished, I felt it was necessary to understand my strengths and weaknesses. My goal was to develop my weaknesses and build my strengths. I felt it was necessary to evaluate myself so that I could better facilitate my learnings. It will help develop the gap between where I am now and where I want to go. In essence we are trying to develop an *understanding*, acquiring the *skill* and *attitude*, and the *value* necessary to our learning. We combined material provided by Larry Lottier, classroom articles, and Sara's critical analysis of me.

Strengths: *Tendencies:*

Decisive   Causing action
Inquisitive   Questioning the status quo
Self-assured   Taking authority
Competitive   Causing trouble
Quick
Self-reliant   *Weaknesses:*
Calculated
Communicator   Become a loner
Restrained   Belligerent if individualism is
Analytical   threatened

                                      Enjoys:

                                      Unique assignments
                                      Difficult assignments

Quoted from Larry Lottier, "You are a person who acts positively and directly in the face of opposition. A forceful individual, will take a chance and may even overstep prerogatives."

The self-evaluation has provided me with the direction necessary to facilitate my learnings.

Listening: Goal is to develop active listening techniques to enhance motivational and group decision skills.

Listening is a tool that will be a beneficial quality through-out my entire life. It is necessary to maintain proper listening qualities so that I can more effectively understand the people that I will be working with.

"Listening is not a passive function, but rather one that demands your full energy." The stated quote is from material provided by Dana.

To increase my *skills* and *attitude* for listening to people, I employed these listening techniques:

Stop talking
Show that you want to listen

Remove distractions
Put the talker at ease
Empathize
Be patient
Hold your response
Avoid criticism
Ask questions
Stop talking

Application: Sara and I attended three parties and simply applied the listening techniques; to our surprise, they were very effective. We also applied the techniques to all our classes and the BAM lectures, for which they have been working.

Verification: Sara and I gained the ability to better listen to people. Also, Larry Lottier said that the best executives are the ones who listen the best.

The third part of our learning was motivation. We felt that it was important to know what we liked and didn't like. This was accomplished through our self-evaluations. Motivation is important because management is the art of delegation—getting work done through others. Thus by understanding our personal strengths and weaknesses, we are better able to motivate others. To motivate people, you have to set the proper climate, listen to the people, and understand what they want.

To date, we have increased our listening skills and understanding of ourselves. All those elements are an important part to understanding motivation.

I claimed responsibility for a large motivational project. At the T.K.E. fraternity the officers were elected in November of every year.

Problem: A senior could not be president.
Goal: To change the election date.
End Result: The election date was changed to the first week of every April. I motivated enough people in the T.K.E. house to understand the importance of changing the date. The new by-law was approved.
Verification: Tom Eboli, president.

Group Decisions and Problem Solving is the final area of our learning contract. As evidenced in our motivational section, a group of people at the T.K.E. were motivated by me. However, that was only the first part of this section. The second part is problem solving or more specifically synergy. As we know, synergy is a group of people having the ability to arrive at an equitable solution.

We combined our first three areas of learnings and applied them to the final area of problem solving. In order to effectively problem solve, an individual should know his limitations and area of expertise, be a good listener, and be able to motivate a group in his area of expertise.

To finalize the problem-solving section, I called my friend John Canarsa and asked if he would be willing to give me a tour of Human Synergistics, the company he works for.

John gave me a tour and explained the importance of synergy to me. Human Synergistics offers its services to companies that are having management problems. In essence it provided me with a greater understanding of group decisions and problem solving. Synergy is a growing area of management, and it is necessary that managers understand the concept of group problem solving. There is a great deal of power in group decisions.

Verification: My visit to Human Synergistics on March 9, 1985.

■ SELECTION 11
Virginia Commonwealth University: "The Adult Learner"

☐ Rosemary Caffarella has been using learning contracts (she calls them "learning plans") for several years in her graduate courses in adult education at the University of Maine and, more recently, at Virginia Commonwealth University, in Richmond. She presents the learners with required objectives for each course, but the learners can modify them, add to them, or omit them in order to take into account their previous experience and education and their special needs and interests through negotiation with her. Students do not contract for grades, but Caffarella makes clear at the outset the criteria by which she will evaluate the evidence of accomplishment of the objectives in awarding grades.

This selection presents two contracts for the course "The Adult Learner," which illustrate the flexibility of the contract learning process in accommodating individual differences in pursuing common subject matter content.

This selection was submitted by Rosemary Caffarella, professor of adult education in the School of Education at Virginia Commonwealth University.

Of special interest:

☐ Providing learner initiative within the framework of prescribed course requirements.
☐ Accommodating individual differences in acquiring similar content.

Learning Plan

Suzanne R.

Objectives	Learning Strategies and Resources	Evidence of Accomplishment	Criteria and Means of Validating Evidence	Time Schedule
A. Define from an analytical perspective the concept of adulthood.	1. Five required periodical readings on adulthood/adult development. 2. Evaluation of the Van Hoosen/Worth text. 3. Required readings. 4. In-class activities.	1. Submission of five annotated bibliographies. 2. Submission of a critique/reaction paper. 3. Active class participation. 4. Active class participation.	1. Bibliographies will be clear, concise representations in the required format; validation by professor. 2. Clear, concise evaluation of the text; validation by professor. 3. Active and informed contributions in class; validation by professor and students. 4. (Same as #3)	2/1/83
B. Describe major sociological, psychological, physiological, and environmental factors which make adults distinct from earlier developmental periods.	1. Required readings. 2. In-class activities.	1. Active class participation. 2. Active class participation.	1. Active and informed contributions in class; validation by professor and students. 2. (Same as #1)	
C. Develop an understanding of the theoretical base of adult development and its relationship to adults as learners.	1. Five required periodical readings on adulthood/adult development (same as A. #1).	1. Submission of five annotated bibliographies.	1. Bibliographies will be clear, concise representations in the required format; validation by professor.	2/1/83

Objective	Learning Activities	Evaluation	Criteria	Date
	2. Required text readings.	2. Active participation.	2, 3, & 4. Active and informed contributions in class; validation by professor and students.	
	3. In-class activities.	3. Active participation.		
	4. "The Great Debate."			
D. Interpret and distinguish the major schools of learning theory and their proponents, especially those focusing on adults as learners.	1. Five required periodical readings on learning in adulthood.	1. Submission of five annotated bibliographies.	1. Bibliographies will be clear, concise representations in the required format; validation by professor.	3/1/83
	2. Required text readings.	2. Active participation.	2 & 3. Active and informed contributions in class; validation by professor and students.	
	3. In-class participation.	3. Active participation.		
E. Identify and analyze current models of adult motivation for learning.	1. Three additional periodical readings on motivation/compliance in health education with adults.	1. Submission of three additional annotated bibliographies.	1. Bibliographies will be clear, concise representations in the required format; validation by professor.	3/29/83
	2. Required text readings.	2. Active participation.	2 & 3. Active and informed contributions in class; validation by professor and students.	
	3. In-class activities.	3. Active participation.		
F. Describe and interpret present data available on the effect of aging on the functions/processes of learning.	1. Three periodical readings on aging and learning specifically with old age (additional).	1. Submission of three additional annotated bibliographies.	1. Bibliographies will be clear, concise representations in the required format; validation by professor.	4/5/83
	2. Required text readings.	2. Active participation.	2 & 3. Active and informed contributions in class; validation by professor and students.	
	3. In-class activities.			

Learning Plan, Cont'd.

Suzanne R.

Objectives	Learning Strategies and Resources	Evidence of Accomplishment	Criteria and Means of Validating Evidence	Time Schedule
G. Describe self as an adult person in terms of the life-cycle perspective and as a learner.	1. Personal reevaluation of self as adult learner.	1. Submission of postscript to "I, An Adult Learner" paper.	1. Paper will be clear, honest, and concise; validation by professor.	4/26/83
	2. Interview task.	2. Submission of interview report and class presentation.	2. Presentations, both written and oral, will follow required format; validation by professor. Reports will be clear, well thought through.	4/12/83
	3. Required readings.	3. Active participation.	3 & 4. Active and informed contributions in class; validation by professor and students.	
	4. In-class activities.	4. Active participation.		
H. Describe implications of concepts and theories related to adult development for the education of adults.	1. Interview task (same as G. #2).	1. Submission of interview report and class presentation.	1. Presentations, both written and oral, will follow required format; reports will be clear, well thought through; validation by professor.	4/12/83

2. Five additional periodical readings focusing on education of the coronary bypass patient.	2. Submission of five additional annotated bibliographies.	2. Bibliographies will be clear, concise representations in the required format; validation by professor.
3. Develop a list of educational considerations in teaching adult coronary bypass patients.	3. Submission of a written list of educational considerations and brief class presentation.	3. List will imply use of concepts and theories of learning and adult development; validation by ADE 601 professor and by nursing professor dealing with patient education. Class presentation will be brief and comprehended by nonnursing peers.
4. Required readings.	4. Active participation.	4 & 5. Active and informed contributions by class; validation by professor and students.
5. In-class activities.	5. Active participation.	

Learning Plan

Sylvia E.

Objectives	Learning Strategies and Resources	Evidence of Accomplishment	Criteria and Means of Validating Evidence	Time Schedule
1. Analytically define the concept of adulthood.	1. Required readings.	1. Active contribution during class discussions.	1. Validation of contribution to discussion by class/instructor.	Prior to and during each class period.
	2. Five required journal readings.	2. Written summary/annotation of each article for use by class in bibliography.	2. Brief, concisely written and typed annotations. Validated by class and instructor.	10/9/84
	3. Conduct 3 interviews.	3. Written reports.	3. Written reports will clearly illustrate subject's present life stage and changes associated with that stage. Validation by team members and instructor.	11/6/84 11/13/84
	4. Personal diary.	4. Written weekly diary reflecting in-class experiences and comprehension of course.	4. Introspectively written in an expressive, personal manner, demonstrating personal growth and accomplishment of course objectives. Validation by instructor and self.	12/4/84
2. Describe the major physiological, psychological, sociological, and anthropological factors that make adults distinct from earlier developmental levels.	1. Required readings.	1. Active contribution during class discussions.	1. Validation of contribution to discussion by class/instructor.	Prior to and during each class period.
	2. Five required journal readings.	2. Written summary/annotation of each article for use by class in bibliography.	2. Brief, concisely written and typed annotations. Validated by class and instructor.	

	3. Conduct 3 interviews.	3. Written reports.	3. Written reports will clearly illustrate subject's present life stage and changes associated with that stage. Validation by team members and instructor.	11/6/84 11/13/84
	4. Personal diary.	4. Written weekly diary reflecting in-class experiences and comprehension of course. I'll be interested in reviewing your reflections!	4. Introspectively written in an expressive, personal manner, demonstrating personal growth and accomplishment of course objectives. Validation by instructor and self.	12/4/84
3. Compare and contrast the various theories underlying adult development.	1. Required readings.	1. Active contribution during class discussions.	1. Validation of contribution to discussion by class/instructor.	Prior to and during each class period.
	2. Five required journal readings.	2. Written summary/annotation of each article for use by class in bibliography.	2. Brief, concisely written and typed annotations. Validated by class and instructor.	
	3. Conduct 3 interviews.	3. Written reports.	3. Written reports will clearly illustrate subject's present life stage and changes associated with that stage. Validation by team members and instructor.	11/6/84 11/13/84
	4. Personal diary.	4. Written weekly diary reflecting in-class experiences and comprehension of course.	4. Introspectively written in an expressive, personal manner, demonstrating personal growth and accomplishment of course objectives. Validation by instructor and self.	12/4/84

Learning Plan, Cont'd.

Sylvia E.

Objectives	Learning Strategies and Resources	Evidence of Accomplishment	Criteria and Means of Validating Evidence	Time Schedule
4. Describe myself as an adult person in terms of the life-cycle perspective.	1. Required readings.	1. Active contribution during class discussions.	1. Validation of contribution to discussion by class/instructor.	Prior to and during each class period.
	2. Five required journal readings.	2. Written summary/annotation of each article for use by class in bibliography.	2. Brief, concisely written and typed annotations. Validated by class and instructor.	10/9/84
	3. Conduct 3 interviews.	3. Written reports.	3. Written reports will clearly illustrate subject's present life stage and changes associated with that stage. Validation by team members and instructor.	11/6/84 11/13/84
	4. Personal diary.	4. Written weekly diary reflecting in-class experiences and comprehension of course.	4. Introspectively written in an expressive, personal manner, demonstrating personal growth and accomplishment of course objectives. Validation by instructor and self.	12/4/84
	5. Attend "Dealing with the Stress of Change" Workshop—Women's Resource Center, U. of R. Substituted Brown Bag Workshops.	5. Summarize in writing the thrust of the workshop and how it applied to my own daily life.	5. Report will be well organized and clearly written. Summary will illustrate clearly the impact of stress and change in the adult life cycle. Instructor validation. Seminar instructor validation.	10/16/84

	Evidence	Validation	Date
6. Conduct panel discussion of the stress of change in middle adulthood.	6. In-class panel presentation with guest panelists who have been widowed or divorced and remarried.	6. Well-organized and good facilitator/moderator techniques used. Validation by class members and instructor.	10/23/84
5. Describe and analyze the implications of the concepts and theories related to adult development for the education of adults.			
1. Required readings.	1. Active contribution during class discussions.	1. Validation of contribution to discussion by class/instructor.	Prior to and during each class period.
2. Five required journal readings.	2. Written summary/annotation of each article for use by class in bibliography.	2. Brief, concisely written and typed annotations. Validated by class and instructor.	10/9/84
3. Conduct 3 interviews.	3. Written reports.	3. Written reports will clearly illustrate subject's present life stage and changes associated with that stage. Validation by team members and instructor.	11/6/84 11/13/84
4. Personal diary.	4. Written weekly diary reflecting in-class experiences and comprehension of course.	4. Introspectively written in an expressive, personal manner, demonstrating personal growth and accomplishment of course objectives. Validation by instructor and self.	12/4/84

ACCEPTED! YOUR LEARNING PLAN LOOKS VERY GOOD AND INTERESTING. WE'LL ALL BE INTERESTED IN HEARING THE PANEL YOU BRING IN AS GUESTS. ENJOY.

Rosemary S. Caffarella

■SELECTION 12
Brandon University: "Business Communications"

☐ The instructor of this course at Brandon University, Manitoba, Canada, prescribes the objectives, strategies, and evidence for a C-grade contract ("Base Assignment") but then provides a wide range of options for B- or A-level contracts. The initiative for constructing B- and A-level contracts is left with the learners, but they must negotiate with the instructor for acceptance of their contracts. The guidelines for B- and A-level contracts are reproduced here, followed by the prescribed C-level, or base-assignment, contract.

This selection was provided by J. P. Fahey, instructor in business communications at Brandon University.

Of special interest:

□   The combination of a highly structured, prescribed contract for a C grade with a wide range of freedom for the learners in constructing contracts for a B or an A.
□   A description of acceptable types of evidence.

Competency-Based Evaluation Contract
A-Grade Contract

Plan #1 for a Grade of A	**Plan #2 for a Grade of A**

1. Complete the Base Assignment.

2. Complete at least 2 learning objectives.

3. Complete at least 1 more learning objective. If you choose to complete only 1 more learning objective, the project should be worthy of an A grade. ("Worthy" is subject to the discretion of the instructor.)

1. Complete the Base Assignment.

2. If you have any ideas for an appropriate project for this class that would be of more benefit to you, it is your option to identify this and negotiate an acceptable grade level for this project with the instructor.

IF AT ANY TIME YOU WISH TO RENEGOTIATE THIS CONTRACT FOR A LOWER GRADE, YOU HAVE THE OPTION TO DO SO.

SIGNED _____   SIGNED _____
              Learner   Instructor

DATE _____

Competency-Based Evaluation Contract
B-Grade Contract

Plan #1 for a Grade of B	Plan #2 for a Grade of B

1. Complete the Base Assignment.

2. *LEARNING OBJECTIVES*

(a) Present evidence (see Note below) on one of the chapter topics presented in the text.
OR
(b) Present evidence from another source on an approved topic.
OR
(c) Take part in a panel discussion/debate on a relevant topic (e.g., "Should titles be retained in letter writing?" or "How to Streamline Your Letters").
AND
(d) Any other project approved by the instructor.

1. Complete the Base Assignment.

2. *LEARNING OBJECTIVES*

If you have any ideas for an appropriate project for this class that would be of more benefit to you, it is your option to identify this and negotiate an acceptable grade level for this project with the instructor.

NOTE: EVIDENCE MAY BE (A) *WRITTEN:* BOOK REVIEW, ESSAY, CASE STUDY, PROPOSAL, INTERVIEW, QUESTIONNAIRE, SURVEY, COMPARE/CONTRAST, ETC.; (B) *VISUAL:* CHART, TABLE, DIAGRAM, SLIDE PRESENTATION, AUDIOVISUAL PRESENTATION, POSTER, PICTOGRAM, ETC.: (C) *AUDITORY:* SPEECH, SKIT, DEBATE, TAPED INTERVIEW, PANEL DISCUSSION, ETC.

If at any time you wish to renegotiate this contract for a higher or lower grade, you have the option to do so.

SIGNED _____   SIGNED _____
            Learner   Instructor

DATE _____

Competency-Based Evaluation Contract
C-Grade Contract
Base Assignment: Business Communications Letter Writing

Objectives	Strategies	Evidence
At the end of the course the student will be able:		
1. To define a *writing objective.* To define a *primary objective.*	The student will read and study the definitions of a writing objective and a primary objective in "How to Write in Ways That Work" until (s)he understands the meaning and is able to recall the definitions' meanings and intentions.	1. The student will write the definitions. 2. The student will define a writing objective and/or a primary objective at given times.
2. To be able to recognize the primary writing objective.	The student will be given at least 10 unfamiliar letters and will be asked to "pick out" the primary writing objective in each.	The student will have correctly identified the primary writing objectives in all of the letters given.
3. To be able to state a basic plan (method) in outline form for all letters in order to help the student become a better-organized, more effective letter writer.	The student will read and comprehend "Making a Plan," pp. 16–18 of *Improving Communication as a Transmitter.*	The student will write a "Basic Information Block." The student will verbally state the three basic blocks and the purpose of each in one of the following ways: (a) in front of the class to classmates, (b) to the instructor alone, (c) in a small discussion group.

	Objective	Criteria
4.	To be able to use Blicq's block effectively for a letter of complaint.	The student will respond in writing with a complaint letter written according to the Blicq outline given in class.	The student's letter will state the summary statement first, the complaint in the second paragraph, and the action in the concluding paragraph; the letter will be effective according to the instructor's evaluation criteria.
5.	To be able to organize thoughts into formats for at least 3 types of letters used by the student at work, or according to his/her need or according to his/her choice.	The student will design a format for each type of letter chosen (see "Letter Writing Formats") and design at least 1 letter for each.	The student will submit the designs for the letter types chosen to the instructor for evaluation; or the student will present the design formats to the class (either in writing or orally) for evaluation; or another method chosen by the student and accepted by the instructor.
6.	To be able to explain and understand basic punctuation, grammar, and form.	The student, as part of a group, will present the class with one segment/topic as stated in the objective.	The student will present the topic in a form approved by the group and the instructor (i.e. written presentation, questionnaire, skit, class test, etc.).
7.	To be able to write a good business letter without prior knowledge of the topic, given a time limit.	The student will be given 3 unfamiliar topics for reply.	The student will write a reply for each of the 3 topics, within a stated time limit.

THIS IS A C-GRADE CONTRACT. THE OBJECTIVES ARE *NOT* RENEGOTIABLE. *STRATEGIES* & *EVIDENCE* ARE RENEGOTIABLE SUBJECT TO APPROVAL BY THE INSTRUCTOR. YOU HAVE THE OPTION *NOT* TO ACCEPT THE CONTRACT IF YOU WISH TO FAIL THE COURSE, AUDIT THE COURSE, OR RENEGOTIATE FOR A D-GRADE. IF YOU WISH TO TRY TO MEET THE OBJECTIVES OF *AT LEAST* A C-GRADE, PLEASE SIGN BELOW.

DATE _____

SIGNED _____ Student

SIGNED _____ Instructor

■SELECTION 13
Augusta College: A Student-Option Grade Contract

☐ This is an example of a different kind of negotiation between a learner and an instructor. Eight learning activities are prescribed, and the learner is given some choices about how and at what depth they will be carried out and what percentage each will contribute to the final grade—subject, of course, to negotiation with the instructor.

This selection was provided by Mary Anne Christenberry, instructor in the course "The Development of the Young Child," in the School of Education at Augusta College, Augusta, Georgia.

Of special interest:

□ The use of prescribed learning activities, the learner being given limited options.
□ The placing of a percentage value on the options by negotiation.

Contract: Education 603
"The Development of the Young Child"

It is agreed by _____ and by the instructor of EDU603 that the following tasks will be satisfactorily completed by _____ for the grade _____ .

The Terms of the Contract

1. I will take the EXAMS as scheduled in the course outline, realizing that the grades earned on the exams will constitute _____% of my final grade.
2. I will attend at least _____ class sessions. I realize that class attendance and participation may be taken into account in the final evaluation of the course.
3. I will submit a CHILD STUDY prepared according to guidelines supplied by the instructor, typed, and submitted to the instructor by _____ for _____% of my final grade.
4. I will prepare, research, and write individual/group reports concerning _____ theorists/researchers on the dates specified in the class schedule. I will also present them orally on the following dates:
   Report #1 _____ Report #5 _____
   Report #2 _____ Report #6 _____
   Report #3 _____ Report #7 _____
   Report #4 _____ Report #8 _____
   These reports will account for _____% of my final grade.
5. I will read and report on at least _____ readings from literature such as journals, book chapters, etc., for _____% of my final grade.
6. I will read the textbook as indicated in the syllabus and will participate actively in class discussions, realizing that this will be taken into account in the final evaluation of this course.
7. I will prepare and lead class discussion from assigned sections of the supplementary text, *Annual Editions,* on the following date(s):
   _____ , _____ , _____ , _____ .

This(these) report(s) will account for _____% of my final grade.

8.   Attached is the plan for the individual project I will

_____

   plan/begin/complete

Note: Your project will include:
     1.   Statement of the problem (question, interest)
     2.   Your plan of action
     3.   Summary of the project
              or
           Plan for implementation
     4.   Evaluation to be used in the project
     5.   Further implications for the future of your project (if applicable)

THIS CONTRACT MAY BE REVISED and/or RENEGO-TIATED with the mutual consent and approval of the instructor and the student by _____ if indicated.

                    Signed _____ , _____
                              Student   Date
                    Signed _____ , _____
                              Instructor   Date

Observations and Reflections

Two key concepts run through the contemporary literature on higher education: learner involvement and individualized instruction (Chickering and Associates, 1981; Fairchild, 1977; Knowles, 1969; Milton and Associates, 1978; Newman, 1971; Perry, 1977; Runkel and others, 1969; Vermilye, 1975). American colleges and universities, however, have a long tradition of emphasis on teacher control and didactic instruction; hence the accelerating growth in recent years of nontraditional programs of higher education (Commission on Non-Traditional Study, 1973; Gould and Cross, 1972; Houle, 1973; Keeton and Tate, 1978; Milton, 1972; Vermilye, 1972, 1974). But the selections in this chapter give evidence that innovative teachers are trying to find ways to involve learners and individualize instruction in traditional academic campus-based courses, and they suggest that contract learning is one of the most effective (and efficient) ways to accomplish these ends.

The aspects of the contracting process in which the instructors represented in this chapter consistently maintain control are in the prescription of objectives and the evaluation of learning (grading). All of this chapter's examples allow for some degree of initiative by the learners in proposing what strategies and resources they will use in achieving the objectives. And all of them except Augusta College provide for some degree of freedom for the learners to modify or formulate the objectives. The point at which teacher control is most protected is in determining the final grade, but even here, all examples show some degree of participation by the learners in specifying or requesting a grade.

In all cases a negotiation relationship between learners and instructors is established. This may be the deepest wedge of all in the traditional academic bastion, for it begins to redefine the role of the instructor away from totally controlling didactic teacher toward facilitator of learning who is willing to share control to some degree. But it also places a heavy responsibility on the instructor to be open and clear about what the boundaries of freedom are (and why) and what his or her criteria for making evaluative judgments will be.

All in all, this chapter leaves me feeling empathic for the instructors who are trying to be facilitators of learning in a traditional academic environment but grateful that they are trying.

 SIX

Clinical Courses, Graduate Assistantships, and Internships

■ *Several persons have told me that the single most useful application of contract learning in their practice is in experiential learning situations, such as practicums, clinical placements, and internships, in which the learning is often unstructured. A learning contract provides a structure and ensures that all parties involved—often a faculty adviser, a field supervisor, and the learner—will be equally clear about the educational outcomes the field experience is intended to produce. Additionally, field supervisors frequently perceive their responsibilities to be limited to supervising the job of the learner, and the learning contract makes explicit what the field supervisor's educational responsibilities are.*

In my own practice, when a field supervisor is involved, I negotiate with the learner a contract that specifies (1) what learning objectives are to be accomplished, (2) how the learner will make use of the resources of the supervisor, co-workers, clients, documents, and other people at the work site, (3) what evidence of accomplishment of the objectives the student will assemble, and (4) how the evidence will be validated. When the learner and I agree on the contract, we initial it. The learner then takes it to the supervisor, reviews the contract with the supervisor, and asks for his or her suggestions. When they agree, the supervisor initials the contract—thus making it a three-way contract. My own experience is that this process greatly enhances the educational value of a field experience.

The first two selections in this chapter provide case descriptions of the use of contract learning in a clinical course at the McMaster University School of Nursing and in a graduate assistantship at the Ontario Institute for Studies in Education. The third selection describes procedures developed at Cornell University for making the most of an internship.

150

■ SELECTION 14
McMaster University School of Nursing: A Clinical Course in Guided Nursing Practice

□ Both the School of Nursing and the School of Medicine at McMaster University, in Hamilton, Ontario, have been pioneers in the use of competency-based education and contract learning in professional education. In my *Andragogy in Action* (Knowles and Associates, 1984) there is a description of the School of Medicine program. This selection presents the instructions students are given for preparing a contract in a clinical (nonclassroom) course in the fourth year of the nursing education program. Notice that although the learning objectives ("Expectations of Students on Completion") are given in the syllabus, emphasis is placed on self-directed learning for both personal and professional growth. Criteria are provided for differentiating A, B, and C grade levels. The contract is negotiated with the faculty adviser. An example of an A-level contract is included.

This selection was provided by Mary Buzzell, a member of the faculty of the McMaster University School of Nursing.

Of special interest:

□ A detailed description of the course's expectations of the students, course requirements, and process for constructing a contract.
□ Criteria for contracting for a grade.

McMaster University
School of Nursing
Guided Nursing Practice
N4J7/4K7

Expectations of Students Entering Year IV

The student is an adult learner who:

1. can function clinically without direct faculty supervision.
2. can describe goals, interests, and learning needs for Year IV.
3. can understand that self-directed learning and evaluation require appropriate use of a variety of resources.

Structural "Givens" for Clinical Course (N4J7/4K7)

The student will:

1. establish and carry out a learning contract to meet course expectations and personal goals.
2. have clinical practice 24 hours weekly which involves continuous responsibility for patient care. Clinical time is to be negotiated with clinical staff for any shift on any day except class day.
3. arrange for regular meetings with liaison faculty member and clinical personnel.
4. explore a selected concept in theoretical depth and demonstrate application of this concept.
5. plan interaction with a variety of resource people, for example, adviser, clinical personnel.
6. participate in clinical seminars during one term.
7. participate in a group teaching seminar to be organized through a student committee with a faculty resource person.

Expectations of Students on Completion of N4J7/4K7

The terminal objectives of the B.Sc.N. program were used as a base for developing the expectations of N4J7/4K7. This course should allow the student to strengthen two core components of a professional person: self-development and professional competence. The behaviors outlined under each component constitute the minimal level of achievement for successful completion of the course.

I. *Self-Development*
   A. *Self-Direction*
       The student:
       1. evaluates achievement objectively; describes specific strengths and areas needing further development.
       2. takes initiative in using a variety of resources to meet learning needs and evaluate achievement.
       3. assumes major responsibility for personal learning and contributes to others' learning and development.
       4. plans for constructive use of resources including negotiating for appropriate time and planning the focus of meetings with resource people.
   B. *Assertiveness*
       The student:
       1. maintains an appropriate balance between assertiveness and acceptance of others' ideas and actions.
       2. gives rationale for ideas and actions when challenged.
       3. presents self (including ideas and actions) in a confident but nondefensive and nonthreatening manner.
       4. contributes alternative ideas and/or suggestions for change in situations where some risk may be perceived.
   C. *Uniqueness*
       The student:
       1. appreciates individuality of self and others.
       2. expresses individuality in the application of general principles to a variety of situations.
       3. values and supports the individuality of others in cooperative situations.

D.   *Self-Awareness*
     The student:
     1.   describes level of confidence and reasons for this level.
     2.   uses verbal and nonverbal feedback from others to increase self-awareness and objectivity.
     3.   is sensitive to personal responses and reactions to others and uses this sensitivity to promote self-growth.

II. *Nursing Competence Through Synthesis of Theory and Practice*
     A.   *Interpersonal Relationships*
          The student:
          1.   takes responsibility for maintenance of a group as a system, implying understanding of personal role in groups.
          2.   is flexible in adjusting interaction with others according to expectations while maintaining integrity.
     B.   *Professional Growth*
          The student demonstrates:
          1.   responsibility by
               ■   establishing objectives for provision of service as well as educational needs.
               ■   identifying situations in which patient care takes priority over learning needs and is flexible in altering actions to fit the situation.
          2.   accountability by
               ■   being an informed decision maker who makes decisions, takes actions, and accepts responsibility for consequences of decisions and actions.
               ■   acknowledging patients' rights and being accountable to patients, encouraging the patient to be his or her own advocate.
               ■   recognizing personal responsibility for continuing learning.
     C.   *Nurse's Role (Practice)*
          The student:

1. organizes and provides safe, effective care for a group of patients including appropriate contact with family and community.
2. functions as a responsible team member by maintaining a balance between service needs of the team and the student's educational needs.
3. takes initiative in actively participating in team organization and planning of patient care.
4. understands nursing role in coordinating total patient care and develops beginning skills of coordination.
5. takes responsibility for promoting health and preventing illness through individual, family, and community education.
6. demonstrates an understanding of the "expanded role" of the nurse by application of a variety of skills in clinical practice.

D. *Scholarly Application*
The student:
1. demonstrates application of knowledge by providing rationale for actions.
2. produces in writing a conceptual or theoretical framework that has application in clinical practice. The application may be in written form or in the form of a project. University standards for writing academic papers are to be followed.

The How-To's of Contract Learning

The philosophy and structure of the N4J7/4K7 course are built on the principles of adult learning. The learning contract has been established to help create an atmosphere in which students are free to explore and discover in dialogue and interaction with others. The method acknowledges the need for the learning to have personal involvement and relevance on the part of the learner. It provides the mechanism for self-direction, by the student, as well as attainment of the expectations of the course.

I.   Familiarity with the Givens

The course expectations have just been outlined for you. They serve as a major part of the "game rules," or givens, that you need to become familiar with before beginning to design your individual learning contract. Other "givens" are the modes or already established learning experiences that are common to all of the students in the course. These experiences are not to be construed as the only modes in which strategies for meeting your objectives can be carried out. You are encouraged to be creative in identifying and planning a wide variety of experiences that are "right" for you and your learning needs.

However, the identified modes that each of you will have available and use include:

1.   *Resource people*—for example, peers, clinical personnel, adviser, Year IV faculty, librarian.
2.   *Clinical settings.*
3.   *Seminars.*
    a.   *Clinical seminars* that allow for exploration of theoretical concepts and their clinical application. They also provide an opportunity for individual students to meet specific objectives related to their learning contracts.
    b.   *Group teaching seminars* that provide an opportunity to practice adult learning principles applied to the presentation of learning that has taken place during the year.
4.   *Learning contract*—in itself, the contract will provide each student with an opportunity to focus on identified individual learning needs within the expectations of the B.Sc.N. graduate.

Becoming familiar with the "givens"—the course expectations and the established learning experiences or modes—is the first step in setting up your contract for the year. The adviser and student have both received information on the givens. It is important that when they first meet together, they come to a *common* understanding of these "game rules." In the first session adviser and student should outline their conditions or "givens," that is, time allotment, and so on, so that they can become more familiar with each other.

II. *Personal Objectives*

Once a common understanding and agreement exist around the givens, the student is ready to sit down and identify personal objectives that relate to or go beyond the course expectations. You begin to see yourself within the framework of course givens by identifying your own needs and interests, individual learning patterns, inner resources and competencies, motivation and investment, and commitments or constrictions outside this course. You can also begin to scan the resources outside self, including seminars, clinical setting, library, and so on, that may be available to help meet your objectives.

III. *Learning Objectives*

Having identified your own personal objectives and goals, it is now necessary to combine these with the "givens" including course expectations to develop the *learning* objectives of the contract. By matching your needs and competencies with the expectations, you can design knowledge, skill, and attitude objectives. You don't need to use the wording given in the course expectations. You can put the objectives into your own context, but if you do, please indicate what expectations are covered by your learning objectives. The students' learning objectives are expected to cover all the minimal standard expectations in some form. The objectives should describe what you will *learn,* not what actions you will take.

IV. *Strategies, Evidence, and Criteria*

Once the learning objectives are outlined, it is necessary to identify and describe activities or "strategies" including resources (material and human) that you will employ to accomplish each objective. The more specific you can be in describing the resources and strategies, the more helpful the adviser can be in making further suggestions.

Continue the contract draft by now specifying what evidence you plan to collect to demonstrate accomplishment of your objectives. Include the dates you plan to complete each evidence.

Perhaps the following examples of evidence will stimulate your thinking about what evidence you might accumulate:

Type of Objective	*Examples of Evidence*
Knowledge	Reports of knowledge acquired, as in essays, examinations, oral presentations, audiovisual presentations; annotated bibliographies.
Understanding	Examples of utilization of knowledge in solving problems, as in action projects, research projects with conclusions and recommendations, plans for curriculum change, and so on.
Skills	Performance exercises, videotaped performances, and so on, with ratings by observers.
Attitudes	Attitudinal rating scales; performance in real situations, role playing, simulation games, critical-incident cases, and so on, with feedback from participants and/or observers.[1]

After you have completed the list of evidences, specify what criteria you propose the evidence will be judged by. The criteria should vary according to the type of objective; for example, appropriate criteria for a knowledge objective with a written paper as evidence might include comprehensiveness, depth, precision, and clarity. After you have specified the criteria, indicate the means you propose to use to have the evidence judged by the criteria. For

[1]Knowles, Malcolm S., "Some Guidelines for Contract Learning" (unpublished material).

example, who will read and judge the written paper and why are they qualified to act as judges? How will they record their judgments of the criteria? You may use a wide variety of resources for validation of evidence, including peers, clinical staff, adviser, and so on.

V.   The Final Contract

The contract draft is now completed. Review this draft with three or four of your peers, perhaps from your seminar group. Your peers can act as consultants in providing you with reactions and suggestions. You may wish to revise or adjust your contract in light of inputs from your peers.

The draft contract is now ready to be taken to your adviser for negotiation. You are free to consult your adviser, as necessary, throughout the preparation of the contract. Final negotiations should take place on or before the end of the first week in October. At this time, you negotiate the items that relate to student learning needs, adviser role, and conditions for involvement. Both student and adviser must be very clear and in agreement on all the items outlined. These negotiations lead to the final written and signed contract. The sooner the contract is made, the better, but renegotiation is available, as necessary, at a later date.

Once your contract has been agreed upon, you may begin to carry out the strategies and collect the evidence to meet your objectives. You are encouraged to maintain and seek feedback and input from your adviser throughout, so that he or she can be of assistance to you in meeting your contract.

VI.   Renegotiation

Renegotiation is open, up to two weeks prior to the date of completion agreed upon for evidence in the contract. Renegotiation may take the form of:

a.   adding objectives, strategies, evidence, and criteria for a higher-level contract.

or

b. deleting objectives, strategies, evidence, and criteria for a lower-level contract.

or

c. altering objectives, strategies, evidence, and criteria for the same-level contract (the altered objectives, strategies, evidence, or criteria must maintain *equal weighting* with the original contract).

or

d. altering dates of completion for presentation of evidences.

Both the adviser and student must be in agreement with the new terms outlined in the renegotiated contract, and this new form is to be signed by both.

VII.   Evaluation

Evidence, once collected, is to be submitted for validation as specified in your contract. All contracts for N4J7/4K7 must be completed and grades submitted on or before April 15, 1977.

Any evidence judged not acceptable requires renegotiation. Options open to the student and adviser at this time include the following:

1. Accept a lower grade level for the contract. In case of the C-level contract, this means a D grade.
2. Redo the evidence with newly specified criteria.
3. Defer graduation until the contract is completed.

Selection of the option is based on the confining realities both adviser and student may be under at the time.

VIII.   The B- and A-Level Contracts

As mentioned earlier, the course expectations are the

minimal requirements for C-level achievement. Therefore, all students are expected to meet these givens and fulfill a learning contract that demonstrates this achievement. It is anticipated that many students will wish to contract for a higher level of accomplishment. In that case, B- and A-level contracts should specify learning objectives that describe learnings that would enable the student to perform at a higher level in two or more of the eight given expectations (for example, Assertiveness, Professional Development). A B-level contract can be met by completion of two of the given expectations "in-depth." "In-depth" means that the student develops strategies, evidences, and criteria that demonstrate more comprehensive achievement of the expected behaviors. An A-level contract can be met by completion of four of the given expectations "in-depth."

When writing out the contract, all students must first identify C-level objectives. After they have finished outlining the strategies, evidences, and criteria for this level, they may choose to go on to identifying more "in-depth" objectives for either an A or B level. The difference between the satisfactory C level, the good B level, and the excellent A level will be in the depth of *knowledge, skill,* or *attitude* accomplishments outlined in the contract.

Learning Contract for Course #4J7: Guided Nursing Practice, A-Level

Student ——————————————————————— Adviser ———————

Learning Objectives (include relationship to course expectations)	Learning Resources and Strategies	Evidence of Accomplishment of Objectives	Criteria and Means for Validating Evidence
To explore and clarify my personal philosophy regarding the issue of suicide, considering the following questions: ■ How do other nurses feel about suicide? ■ Is it fair to be critical of nurses who feel anger and even contempt for suicide-attempt patients? ■ Do I as a nurse have a responsibility (morally) to prevent an individual from taking his or her life?	Nursing and medical journal articles. Intensive Care Unit staff. Peers. Interview with Carolyn Milne, Oct. 24. Interview with nurse from liaison unit, Nov. 20.	One-hour discussion period with Carolyn Milne. Cathy Colvin (student in E.R.) will be involved in the discussion to meet her learning needs as well.	Paper to be submitted to C. Milne prior to presentation/discussion.
To increase my knowledge of pharmacology, specifically drugs such as antibiotics and antihypertensives and their effect on the renal system.	Pharmacology texts. Nursing journals. A.V. material on the renal system. Anatomy and physiology texts.	I will present to the Year IV nursing class a case study of a patient in renal failure, placing special emphasis on the medications used in treatment of her overall condition and how these relate to the renal system, Nov. 22.	Class to evaluate both content and style of presentation by filling out evaluation forms handed out prior to session.

Objective	Learning Activities/Resources	Evaluation	Criteria
To demonstrate an ability to engage in the teaching process.	Principles of teaching-learning will be used with **B. K. Redman**, *The Process of Patient Teaching in Nursing* as the major resource.	Same as above.	Same as above.
To gain knowledge and skill in suctioning patients.	Nursing journal articles. Medical surgical texts. ICU manual and staff. After reviewing the above, I will perform the procedure with an ICU grad supervising.	An evaluation form will be filled out by an ICU grad and submitted to Bonnie Reeves.	Criteria will be outlined in the evaluation form.
To learn an efficient system for giving reports on my patients.	Nursing journal articles. Reviewing reporting styles of ICU staff—which are good, which not?	A written format for verbal reporting on patients.	Bonnie Reeves to evaluate.
To gain knowledge and skill in the administration of cardiopulmonary resuscitation.	Nursing literature. C.P.R. seminar. Attendance at C.P.R. class at Mohawk College.	Certificate noting that I have passed the C.P.R. course, Dec. 1 and 2.	Criteria as outlined by course.
To demonstrate an ability to engage in the problem-solving process in caring for a patient with many problems.	Patient's chart. Physical assessment of patient. ICU staff. Texts and nursing journal articles. A patient situation will be selected from the ICU setting and will be analyzed in terms of problems diagnosed.	Written paper.	Adviser to evaluate. Criteria as outlined in "Great Expectations Revised." Additional criteria (more specific) to be submitted with paper.

A. Contract successfully negotiated for a ——— grade.   Student: ———
                                                                Adviser: ———

B. Contract successfully met for a ——— grade.   Student: ———
                                                                Adviser: ———

■ **SELECTION 15**

Ontario Institute for Studies in Education: A Graduate Assistantship

□ So often graduate assistantships are a means for supplying professors with "gofers." In this selection a student takes the initiative in laying out a detailed plan for using his internship to carry out a systematic research project. It starts with a self-diagnosis of learning needs and then spells out the objectives, learning resources and strategies, and evaluation procedures in the contract.

This selection was submitted by William Barnard, who at the time was a member of the faculty of the Department of Adult Education of the Ontario Institute for Studies in Education, in Toronto.

Of special interest:

□   A learner-constructed rating scale for diagnosing learning needs.
□   An A-level contract for converting a graduate assistantship into a learning experience.

Student's Statement of Learning Need

Learning Need: To design a plan for the evaluation of the certificate program (Adult Ed. Dept., OISE) utilizing heuristic research methods.

Competencies Required to Fulfill Learning Need	Personal Assessment P = present level, R = required level		
	Low	Mod.	High
Knowledge of heuristic research	P	R	
Knowledge of heuristic research methods		P	R
Understanding of the certificate program			P R
Understanding of the relationship between quantitative and qualitative research methods	P	R	
Skill in applying heuristic research methods in designing an evaluation of the certificate program	P	R	
An attitude of trust in the value of heuristic research as an evaluative process		P	R

Individual Learning Contract (A-Level)

Learning Need: To design a plan for the evaluation of the certificate program utilizing heuristic research methods.

Learning Objectives	Learning Resources and Strategies	Evidence of Accomplishment	Criteria and Means for Validating Evidence
1. To develop knowledge of heuristic research: ■ Historical perspectives ■ Predominant proponents ■ Basic tenets	Books: Thevenay, *What Is Phenomenology?* Bogdan & Taylor, *Introduction to Qualitative Research Methods* McCall, *Identities and Interactions* Bruyn, *Human Perspective in Sociology* Allport, *Use of Personal Documents in Psychological Science* Georgi, *Psychology as a Human Science* Moustakas, Individuality and Encounter (Chap. 5, "Heuristic Research") Denzin, *The Research Act* Maslow, *The Psychology of Science* Webb, *Unobtrusive Measures* Stewart & Mickunas, *Exploring Phenomelogy* Articles: Dean, John P., et al., "Limitations and Advantages of Unstructured Methods," *An Introduction to Social Research*, 2nd ed., pp. 274–279. Strategies: Reading, reflecting, analyzing, synthesizing, class sessions, experimenting, peer and instructor consultation, reflective journal.	Communicate verbally to class (small group) members an introductory grasp of heuristic research theory. Ask two members of the group to validate the above by signing below.	Able to communicate my ideas verbally about heuristic research with clarity and a moderate degree of completeness. Also, able to express an openness to continue to study and reflect on theory of heuristic research.
2. To develop knowledge of heuristic research methods.	Books and articles: Bogdan & Taylor, *Introduction to Qualitative Research Methods*	Develop a model and plan for applying heuristic research methods to the evaluation of the certificate program	Evaluate the plan for: ■ originality in form and methodology

- Wilson, Steven, "Use of Ethnographic Techniques in Educational Research," *RER*, 47(2), Spring 1977
- Carini, P., *Observation and Description: An Alternative Methodology for the Investigation of Human Phenomena*, 1975
- Bruyn, S., "The Methodology of Participant Observation," *Human Organization*, 21:224–124, 1963
- Rosenthal, R., *Experimenter Effects in Behavioral Research*
- McCall, G. J., & Simmons, L. L., *Issues in Participant Observation*

Strategies:

Reading, reflecting, analyzing, synthesizing, class discussions, peer and instructor consultation.

Develop a model and plan.

in Adult Education (OISE).

Share this plan verbally and in written form with Bill Barnard and ask him to evaluate it.

Evaluation comments:

_____

_____

(more on model itself)

_____

(Signature)

- clarity and logic
- completeness

---

3. To develop understanding of the relationship between quantitative and qualitative research methods.

Books:

- Borg, *Educational Research: An Introduction*
- Campbell & Stanley, *Experimental and Quasi-Experimental Designs for Research*
- Warwick, D. & Lininger, C., *The Sample Survey: Theory and Practice*, 1975
- Patton, M. Q., *Alternative Evaluation Research Paradigms*, 1975
- Worthen & Sanders, *Educational Evaluation: Theory and Practice*

Strategies:

Reading, reflecting, comparing; comparing notes and reflections with another student taking a course in quantitative research.

Assist a fellow student to understand the quantitative approach to research and share with her how that approach relates to the qualitative research methods.

Have this student evaluate my ability to do this.

Evaluation comments:

_____

_____

_____

(more on back of this page, if necessary)

_____

(Signature)

Judge my ability to do this on how well she was able to understand and use my attempt to describe the difference in the two approaches.

Individual Learning Contract (A-Level), Cont.

Learning Objectives	Learning Resources and Strategies	Evidence of Accomplishment	Criteria and Means for Validating Evidence
4. To develop understanding of the certificate program: ■ history of development ■ purposes ■ curriculum ■ admission policies ■ certifying requirements ■ participants	**Resources:** Study annual reports of the certificate program for the years 1967/68, 1968/69, 1969/70, and 1970/71. Interview Lorraine Deason about the early development of the program, the admission policies, and participants. Talk with Rachael (secretary) about the participants, admission policies, and current mailing list. Study early publicity about the certificate program. Study current statement in the OISE Bulletin about the certificate program. **Strategies:** Review the above collected data and compile them into a form (written) which can serve as background information for the information which will be collected as part of the evaluation study of the certificate program.	Compile, in essay form, a statement of the history, purposes, curriculum, admission policies, and certifying requirements of the certificate program as found in the early publicity materials about the program and the annual reports for the first four years of its existence. The essay will also include some information about the students enrolled in the program during the first four years. Do a self-evaluation of this "essay" and keep it to be included with the final report of the evaluation of the certificate program to be completed in April 1978. Evaluation comments: _____ _____ _____ _____ (more on back of this page, if necessary) _____ (Signature)	Evaluate this "essay" for completeness and accuracy, for clarity of statement, and for conciseness.

5.	To learn the skills and implement them in applying heuristic research methods in designing an evaluation plan of the certificate program.	**Books:** Hodgkinson, H., *Improving and Assessing Performance Evaluation in Higher Education* Cooley, W., *Evaluation Research in Education* Borich, G., *Evaluating Educational Programs and Products* Tuckman, *Conducting Educational Research* Harrington, P., *The Future of Adult Education* Parlett, M., *Evaluation as Illumination: A New Approach to the Study of Innovative Programs* (Occ. paper #9, U. of Edinburgh) Popham, W. J., *An Evaluation Guidebook: A Set of Practical Guidelines for the Evaluation Evaluator* **Strategies:** Reading, reflecting, synthesizing, and developing a plan for the evaluation of the certificate program.	Same as for Objective #2.	Same as for Objective #2.
6.	To increase my trust in the value of heuristic research as an evaluative process.	**Books:** PDK National Study Committee on Evaluation, *Educational Evaluation and Decision Making* Weiss, C., *Evaluation Research: Methods of Assessing Program Effectiveness* Borich, G., *Evaluating Educational Programs and Products* **Strategies:** Reflect on the completed plan for the evaluation of the certificate program. Share the plan with Bill Barnard.	Same as for Objectives #1 and #2.	Same as for Objectives #1 and #2.

■ SELECTION 16
Cornell University: Contracting for an Internship

□ The educational value of an internship can be greatly enhanced by involving the faculty adviser, the field supervisor, and the learner in negotiating a contract that spells out the educational objectives to be achieved through the internship, the strategies and resources that will be used to achieve them, and the criteria and procedures by which their accomplishment will be evaluated.

This selection is excerpted from *The Experienced Hand: A Student Manual for Making the Most of an Internship* by Timothy Stanton, formerly director of the Field Study Office of the New York State College of Human Ecology at Cornell University, and Kamil Ali, who initiated an internship at the National Society for Internships and Experiential Education while a junior at Princeton University. The Carroll Press, Cranston, Rhode Island, published the manual in 1982 and has kindly granted permission for the use of portions of it here.

Of special interest:

□   Guidelines for constructing a learning contract for an internship.
□   An example of a contract for an internship in the New York State Assembly.

The Learning Contract

Learning contracts are outlines of what you intend to learn and accomplish while you are on your internship. They are effective tools for gaining agreement between you, your internship supervisor, and your faculty sponsor on your mutual intentions and expectations for the internship, both educational and work-related, as well as on criteria and techniques for grading and evaluation at the internship's conclusion.

Many internship programs require interns and internship supervisors to complete learning contracts before the internship begins in order to be certain that both parties understand and agree to the role and work responsibilities to be carried out by the student and the supervision to be provided by the supervisor. Many college field experience education directors (or faculty who sponsor student interns) utilize learning contracts to develop work and supervision agreements which outline the commitments made by the student and faculty members, thus spelling out the rationale for granting academic credit for the internship.

Since grading of experiential learning is such a complicated and thorny issue, learning contracts are often used to clarify students' learning objectives and determine agreed-upon bases for grading. In all cases, such agreements—no matter who has initiated them—help all three parties in an internship (students, faculty, internship supervisors) develop clear understandings of what they expect of each other at the outset of an internship, understandings they can refer to later if differences or problems arise.

There is a tremendous variety of learning contract forms and designs. If you have a faculty sponsor or are participating in an internship program that requires completing a learning contract, you will probably use their forms. What follows is a learning contract form for use by students who are not required to write such agreements but who wish to obtain agreements on intentions and expectations from their faculty sponsor and internship supervisor before they leave campus or, at least, by the first or second week of the internship.

A sample learning contract appears on the following pages, filled in to give you an idea of what to include in your own contract. Then a blank contract is provided for your own use.

Part I is for the "nuts and bolts" of your internship and should be easy to fill out.

Parts II and III require more thought on your part. Begin by drafting and refining your ideas on blank sheets of paper. Read pertinent sections of this manual for assistance. (For example, to write learning objectives, refer back to the preceding page.) Allow time to show your draft to your faculty sponsor and internship supervisor (by mail, if necessary) for their reactions and revisions. When you have something you feel good about and everyone agrees to, write it into your contract.

Go slowly with this stage, whether you do it on campus before you start your internship or during the first week or two on the job. Thinking through your learning and accomplishing objectives and carefully stating them to yourself and your sponsor and supervisor will help you focus your energies for the internship. As an active, experiential learner, this is your first opportunity to design your own curriculum. Writing up your internship work assignments and stating your expectations for supervision enable you to gain or negotiate a clear understanding of what will happen when you arrive at your workplace. Be thoughtful about it and give yourself enough time—weeks, if you need to use the mails.

Part IV, the signatures signifying agreement, should be simple if you have involved your faculty sponsor and internship supervisor in the preparation of the contract. If you have not involved them, you are likely to have your contract rejected by one or both of them. *Do it right the first time.*

Once you have an agreed-upon contract, you have something to rely on if problems crop up on your internship. If you feel you are not getting the expected supervision on the job, call your supervisor's attention to the contract. If you feel your faculty sponsor is demanding too much or different work than you expected, remind him or her of the contract. If you find yourself changing your objectives or intentions for the internship, take a look at the contract and see if you can figure out why. If you are serious about these changes, amend your contract and seek agreement again from your adviser and supervisor.

Using a learning contract in this way is a good technique for keeping in touch with yourself, your faculty sponsor, and your internship supervisor during an internship and communicating clearly about its most important element—your experience.

Learning Contract

PART I:

A.   Name: _____   Social Security No.: _____

     Campus Address: Home Address:

     _____   _____
                (street)   (street)
     S.U.N.Y., Syracuse, NY 13210   Palmyra, New York 14522
     (city)   (state)   (zip)   (city)   (state)   (zip)

     _____   _____
             (telephone)   (telephone)

     Address while on internship:

          222 E. Pleasant St., Apt. 4
     _____
                          (street)
          Albany, New York 12207
     _____
          (city)   (state)   (zip)
          (518)211-1234
     _____
                          (telephone)

B.   Internship Organization:
     _____Office of Assemblyman, Henry Dinardo, State Assembly_____

     Address: ___New York State Capitol_____

     Telephone: ___(518)678-1000, Ext. 345_____

     Name of Supervisor: Position:
     _____Ingrid Martin_____   ___Senior Political Adviser___

     Your Position: _____Legislative Aide_____

C.   Faculty Sponsor/Adviser: _____Lela Copeland_____

     Department: _____Government_____

     Address: __State University of New York, Syracuse, NY 13210___

     Telephone: ___(315)324-7200_____

D.   Credits to be awarded for   Government   402   15
     internship: Department   Course No.   No. of
                                                            Credits

PART II: THE INTERNSHIP

A.   JOB DESCRIPTION: Describe in as much detail as possible
      your role and responsibilities while on your internship. List
      duties, projects to be completed, deadlines, and so on, if
      relevant.
            Acting as legislative aide, I understand that I will be
      responsible for doing background research on legislative
      issues under consideration in the State Assembly. This
      research will involve library work, telephone inquiries, and
      field visits to constituent agencies and organizations. I will be
      required to write background papers on my findings by
      deadlines to be determined by my supervisor. I will provide
      general assistance in the office—to be determined by my
      supervisor. I will provide clerical assistance in the office—
      telephone answering, reception, messenger service—on an
      occasional basis, as needed. I will work 40 hours per week and
      overtime as needed.

B.   SUPERVISION: Describe in as much detail as possible the
      supervision to be provided: what kind of instruction, assist-
      ance, consultation, and so on, you will receive from whom,
      and so on.
            I will meet weekly with my supervisor to monitor the
      progress of my research and learn about implications and
      results of my findings and the status of relevant legislation. I
      will receive instruction on the use of the State Library from
      other research staff in the office. I will visit the district office
      once every two or three weeks for consultation with its staff
      and constituents on issues under my attention. Bradley Smith,
      office manager, will give me a general orientation and assist
      me as needed in performing general office tasks.

C.   EVALUATION: How will your work performance be evalu-
      ated? By whom? When?
            My work will be evaluated by my supervisor and
      myself in a final consultation session. We will use a standard
      state employee evaluation form as well.

PART III: LEARNING OBJECTIVES/LEARNING
                ACTIVITIES/EVALUATION

A. LEARNING OBJECTIVES: What do you intend to learn
      through this experience? Be specific. Try to use concrete,
      measurable terms.
      (1)   I will be able to describe how public policy is developed
             and enacted in the state legislature.
      (2)   I will understand the role and activities of an
             assemblyman.
      (3)   I will examine and develop an in-depth understanding
             of the involvement of racial minorities in the develop-
             ment of at least two major pieces of social policy
             legislation in the state and the consequences for these
             people as a result of their enactment or lack of enact-
             ment in the legislature.
      (4)   I will develop and practice legislative research and
             report writing.
      (5)   I will improve communication skills—writing, convers-
             ing, and so on.
B. LEARNING ACTIVITIES:
      (1)   On-the-Job: Describe how your internship activities will
             enable you to meet your learning objectives. Include
             projects, research, report writing, conversations, and so
             on, which you will do while working, relating them to
             what you intend to learn.
                    By working in Assemblyman Dinardo's office,
             consulting with my supervisor and co-workers, by
             following legislation from initiation to enactment, by
             researching its need and impact, by visiting constituents,
             by writing reports, by having to communicate clearly by
             telephone, memo, and so on, I will be able to attain my
             learning objectives.
      (2)   Off-the-Job: List reading, writing, contact with faculty
             sponsor, peer group, discussion, field trips, observations,
             and so on, you will make and carry out which will help
             you meet your learning objectives.

During my internship, I will read two books on public policy to be assigned by my faculty sponsor. I will keep a journal of my activities. I will submit three evaluative reports to my sponsor on my progress in my internship. I will talk to other student interns and I will participate in political-social functions.

At the conclusion of my internship, I will write two papers. One will be a self-evaluation of my progress made toward meeting learning objectives. The other will be a term paper (10–15 pages) following the legislative history of a major social policy issue in this year's legislative session and focusing on the involvement of Hispanic Americans in its development and enactment and its probable impact on their lives.

C. EVALUATION: How will you know what you have learned, or that you have achieved your learning objectives? How do you wish to evaluate your progress toward meeting these objectives? Who will evaluate? When? How will a grade be determined? By whom? When?

Evaluation of my progress made toward my learning objectives through this internship will be done in the following ways: Objectives 1, 2, 3, and 5 through my term paper, my self-evaluation report, and conversations with my faculty sponsor, Objective 4 by feedback from my internship supervisor and faculty adviser on reports that I write on my legislative research.

My grade will be determined by my faculty sponsor, who will take into account my self-evaluation and evaluation of my internship supervisor of my work performance.

PART IV: AGREEMENT

This contract may be terminated or amended by student, faculty sponsor, or internship supervisor at any time upon written notice, which is received and agreed to by the other two parties.

Student Signature: _____ Date: _____

Faculty Sponsor: _____ Date: _____

Internship Sponsor: _____ Date: _____

(Copies of this contract should be distributed to all parties.)

Observations and Reflections

The payoff in terms of enhanced learning from the use of contract learning is probably greater in clinical placements and other forms of field experience than in most other settings. This is so because often the focus of the learner is on doing a good job and the focus of the field supervisor is on getting the job done, and what learning takes place is often unplanned and perhaps unrecognized. A learning contract focuses the attention of both parties on the field experience as a learning experience as well as a work experience, and it provides a plan for optimizing the learning outcomes.

I am impressed by several aspects of the contract learning process used at the McMaster University School of Nursing. For one thing, it clearly places the primary responsibility for planning and carrying out the learning on the learner while making equally clear the availability of the faculty members and clinicians as consultants and content resources. It also stresses that nurses are human beings as well as professional practitioners, and it makes provision for including in the contract objectives having to do with personal development as well as those having to do with professional development. Further, it proposes that objectives should be stated in terms of competence development, not just knowledge and skill acquisition, thus ensuring a performance-oriented rather than a test-passing approach to learning. Finally, I was impressed with the extensive use of peers as resources in the sample learning contract.

The graduate assistantship at the Ontario Institute for Studies in Education is the only example in this book in which a learner constructed his own tool for diagnosing his learning needs. It is an especially imaginative plan for converting what is often viewed as strictly a work situation into a learning situation. My hunch is that he learned more about research than most students learn in a rigorous research course.

The example of the internship contracting process at Cornell University provides one of the most concise, specific, and reassuring guidelines for constructing a learning contract that I have seen. It is the only example in this chapter that calls for a three-way negotiation of the contract involving the learner, the faculty sponsor, and the field supervisor.

SEVEN

Professional and Management Development

■ The accelerating pace of change in our society, resulting from the knowledge explosion and the technological revolution, is increasing the rate of obsolescence in many occupations. This phenomenon is especially visible in the health professions and in high-tech industry, but it is also occurring in teaching and other professions.

Accordingly, growing emphasis is being placed on continuing professional education. In fact, consumers of professional services have become so concerned that their providers of professional services keep up to date that a number of state legislatures have passed laws mandating continuing education as a basis for relicensing.

Many professional schools and associations have sought to meet the need for continuing professional development by offering special courses and seminars. But busy practicing professionals often find it difficult, if not impossible, to leave their practices to attend classes, and so contract learning is being adopted increasingly as a preferred mode for accomplishing this purpose.

This chapter presents three examples of this trend. The first selection describes a program of continuing education for physicians sponsored by the University of Southern California Health Sciences Campus. It started as a three-year experiment in 1980, with subsidy from the National Library of Medicine. The second selection describes the faculty development program of Gordon College, in Wenham, Massachusetts, which involves its faculty members on a voluntary basis in constructing and implementing "Individual Development Plans" under the management of an elected faculty development committee. Both these programs place a high degree of responsibility on the learners for assessing their own learning needs and constructing highly individualized learning plans. The third selection describes the Master of

180

Management program of the American Management Association, in New York. This program provides a generic model of the competencies required for performing the role of manager and a rigorous process of needs diagnosis based on that model, but allows a wide span of freedom to the learners in constructing learning plans.

■ SELECTION 17

University of Southern California: Self-Directed Learning Project for Physicians

☐ In 1980 the University of Southern California School of Medicine launched a program of continuing education for physicians, using learning contracts (their terminology: "learning plans") as the basic tool for structuring learning experiences. The process used in developing and monitoring learning plans is described in Knowles and Associates (1984) as follows:

> *Individualized Learning Plans.* Participating physicians develop a brief, but formal, learning plan. The plan clarifies the physician's objectives and outlines a workable course of action. An Education Specialist (from the university) assists physicians in documenting educational needs and constructing manageable learning plans.
> *Information Brokering.* A medical-library-based Information Broker serves participating physicians by linking them to appropriate teaching/learning resources. The broker identifies available community resources to assist physicians in reaching their educational goals. In addition to printed and audiovisual materials, the broker identifies specialized resources—such as consultants, clinics, courses, and equipment—that may be necessary for successful completion of the plan.
> *Peer Resource Groups.* Groups of three to five physicians provide support to the individual members. Although the participants are involved in their own learning projects, they assist one another by information sharing, problem solving, providing technical assistance, and informal personal interaction. The group also serves as a motivating force to complete the self-determined learning plan. Individual physicians maintain direction of their own programs. The peer resource groups meet on a monthly basis over a four-month period [p. 303].

On completion of a learning plan, the evidence of fulfillment of the contract is evaluated by the peer group and the project staff.

An example of a learning plan by a pathologist is provided.

This selection was submitted by Bill Clintworth, project director, Physicians' Self-Directed Learning Project, Health Sciences Campus, University of Southern California, Los Angeles.

Of special interest:

☐ The use of an education specialist, an information broker, and a peer group in developing and carrying out a learning contract.

Postgraduate Medical Education
Learning Plan

Name _____   Specialty ___Pathologist___   Date ___9/24/81___

Overall Goal ___To improve communication between the clinical laboratory and practicing physicians.___

Objectives (What do you want to be able to do?)	Resources/Strategies (How are you going to learn it?)	Evidence of Accomplishment (How will you demonstrate you have learned it?)	Criteria and Means of Validating Evidence (How will you judge your level of performance?)	Target Date
1.0 Implement a method to disseminate information regarding the availability, use, and interpretation of laboratory tests.	1.1 Select a new laboratory test, or several with which you believe practicing physicians are unfamiliar, and determine a method for best presenting the information (lecture, audiotape, bulletin). 1.1.1 Needs assessment information from practicing physicians regarding most unfamiliar lab tests and preferred methods of receiving information. 1.1.2 Consult other medical directors of clinical labs to inquire about methods used for dissemination of information. 1.2 Review resources regarding (a selected) new laboratory test and supervise development of dissemination method.	1.0 Provide an example of the method devised to disseminate information about laboratory tests.	1.0 Collect and interpret feedback from practicing physicians with regard to the helpfulness of the laboratory test information and the usefulness of the communication method.	Jan. 1982
2.0 Identify strategies or techniques that may increase the utility and meaning of lab reports for practicing physicians.	2.1 Review resources regarding lab results reporting. 2.1.1 Literature search articles. 2.1.2 Descriptions of features of computer application designed for laboratory results reporting. 2.1.3 Lab report forms used in other hospitals. 2.1.4 Inquiries of practicing physicians.	2.0 Describe at least three strategies or techniques that could be implemented to make lab reports more meaningful to physicians.	2.0 Have strategies or techniques rated by five practicing physicians on utility, clarity, and relevance.	Jan. 1982

■ SELECTION 18

Gordon College: Individual Development Plans for Faculty Development

☐ In 1976 Gordon College, in Wenham, Massachusetts, instituted a program of faculty development by what it called "growth contracting," supported by a grant from the W. K. Kellogg Foundation. In 1981 the managers of the program decided that the term *contract* implies more legality than they wished to suggest, and so they substituted the term *Individual Development Plan*. The program is managed by an elected faculty development committee, which approves development plans and awards budget requests from a special faculty development fund. Faculty participation is completely voluntary, but it approaches 100 percent.

The program can briefly be described as follows: Each participating faculty member writes a faculty profile that contains an assessment of strengths and weaknesses, a statement of the current faculty role, an assessment of effectiveness in carrying out this role, and a statement of long-range professional and personal goals, typically for a period of three to five years. This profile forms the basis for a series of yearly individual development plans intended cumulatively to implement one's long-range goals. Each plan consists of specific goals for the year, with each goal accompanied by a description of intended means for accomplishment and assessment and a budget request. The faculty member also designates an advisory committee, made up mostly of faculty colleagues, whose purpose is to help the faculty member refine the plan, to give advice during the year of implementation, and to write an assessment of goal accomplishment to accompany the participant's self-assessment at the end of the year. The plan is then submitted to the faculty development committee for approval.

The sample Individual Development Plan (IDP) that follows is from an associate professor of English.

This selection was submitted by R. Judson Carlberg, dean of faculty, Gordon College.

Of special interest:

□ Management of a faculty development program by an elected committee rather than by administrators.
□ Use of faculty profiles as a basis for self-diagnosis of learning needs.
□ Provision of financial assistance through a fund originally provided by a foundation and now built into the college budget.

Individual Development Plan

_____ Associate Professor of English

I. Relation of Plan to Profile

My goals for 1980–81 continue to be based on my original interests at the outset of my IDP writing with the natural sophistication and honing which come with the passing of years and the gaining of understanding.

II. Individual Plan for Growth

Goal A:

To continue the development of a strategy and approach for the teaching of freshman writing which will best serve the Gordon student especially in the area of remedial and developmental writing skills and will keep abreast of the new materials, literature, and methods in the field.

1. *Means of Accomplishment:*
    I will attend the annual meeting of the Conference on College Composition and Communication, held this year in Dallas, Texas. This meeting is always valuable in the exposure to plans used in other schools, to alternative strategies, to national testing patterns, and to other constantly changing areas in the field of composition.
    Means of Assessment:
    As always is the case when I return from a national conference, I will write a report on the sessions attended and submit a copy to those members of my committee and my department who might be interested.
2. *Means of Accomplishment:*
    To read in the field, especially materials available to members of the NCTE (National Council of Teachers of English) and the CCCC.

Means of Assessment:
To incorporate such ideas and approaches in the classroom to gauge student reaction by discussion and by standardized form.

3. *Means of Accomplishment:*
To work especially with the area of developmental English to offer my services either to a newly planned developmental program or for severe student needs as they arise.
Means of Assessment:
By implementing ideas for student tutoring and/or individual help and seeing the student move back into the mainstream of the course.

Budget Request

Membership in NCTE and CCCC (allied organizations)	$ 35.00
Dallas meeting	
Travel	300.00
Room (3 nights)	90.00
Food (3 days)	45.00
TOTAL FOR GOAL A	$470.00

Goal B:

To continue to develop knowledge, training, and understanding of the principles and practice of oral interpretation of literature, especially as it pertains to the performance and direction of readers' theater.

1. *Means of Accomplishment:*
To continue directing the Princemere Readers and experiment with movement, memorization, expanded scripts, and other methods of performance which will move beyond where we presently are. The 1980–81 schedule will focus on the works of C. S. Lewis.

Means of Assessment:
The students themselves and the quality of the performances as well as the reaction of the audiences will tell the success of these new methods and approaches.

2. *Means of Accomplishment:*
    To change and expand my two present oral interpretation courses into three courses and to include new techniques and to allow for more student input into course content and evaluation.
    Means of Assessment:
    The students will judge the effectiveness of the course and of the participation in activities which are intended for their growth.

3. *Means of Accomplishment:*
    To conduct a limited number of guided studies in the performance of literature and to cooperate with other courses, notably those in education, in introducing individuals to the area of oral performance.
    Means of Assessment:
    Again, the students will provide the best basis for judgment, and their performance, as has been the case in the past, will be the very best means of assessment.

4. *Means of Accomplishment:*
    To attend the annual meeting of the Speech Communication Association and of the Religious Speech Communication Association in New York in November. Since I was just appointed national chairperson of the oral interpretation division of the RSCA and am responsible for putting programs, and so on, together, this is an area of growth hitherto unknown to me.
    Means of Assessment:
    I will, as always, write a session-by-session account of the meetings and will also show tangible evidence of my committee and divisional work in the RSCA.

5. *Means of Accomplishment:*
    I will invite a visiting scholar on oral interpretation to Gordon College. This person will conduct a workshop in

techniques of reading and performance as well as hold a reading hour in the evening.
Means of Assessment:
The whole student body will be invited to the workshop and the reading hour. The committee will be informed of these events and may attend.

Budget Request

Membership dues in the SCA and RSCA	$ 35.00
Honorarium for visiting scholar in oral interp.	100.00
TOTAL FOR GOAL B	$135.00

Goal C:

To continue reading and researching the subject of "Methodism and the English Novel" toward the production of a manuscript.

1. *Means of Accomplishment:*
   To accumulate more books and articles and to begin to interface my sources into a thesis statement.
   Means of Assessment:
   My resource person, Dr. Bishop, will guide me in the proper direction and let me know when and where I am off the track.

Budget Request

Purchase of Wesley books and Xeroxing of articles	$ 70.00
TOTAL FOR GOAL C	$ 70.00

III. Proposed Evaluation Committee

1. Russell Bishop—Goal C
2. John Burgess—Goal B, #3
3. Bernice White, Southwestern College in Memphis—Goal B

IV.   Summary of Budget Requests

Participant: _____
Fiscal Year of the Plan: 1980–81
Individual Development Fund __X__ Leave of Absence Fund _____

Cost Categories

1.	Freshman writing aids	$470.00
2.	Oral interpretation	135.00
3.	Research on Wesley and literature	70.00
	TOTAL BUDGET REQUEST	$675.00

■ SELECTION 19
American Management Association's Master of Management Program

☐ Since 1981 the American Management Association (AMA) has offered a Master of Management degree program. Although this is a graduate-degree program, admission to it is limited to people already in management positions, and the program of study is integrated with the learners' worklife, so that it seems to fit better under the label "management development" than the label "academic classroom courses."

The program is organized around a model of eighteen generic management competencies that are grouped into four "clusters" as follows:

Goal and Action Management Cluster
   Efficiency orientation
   Proactivity
   Concern with impact
Directing Subordinates Cluster
   Use of unilateral power
   Developing others
   Spontaneity
Human Resource Management Cluster
   Use of socialized power
   Managing group process
   Positive regard
   Accurate self-assessment
   Self-control
   Stamina and adaptability
Leadership Cluster
   Self-confidence
   Conceptualization
   Logical thought
   Use of oral presentation

Applicants to the program are assessed regarding their level of development of these competencies through performance assessment exercises and special tests. Six weeks after the initial assessment, applicants return to learn the results in a Feedback Week. The learners then design a competency-development plan (CDP) with the aid of their faculty advisers and implement it at their own pace, using primarily the resources of their work sites but also using study groups, reading, and courses at other institutions. Program completion requires use of the competencies on the job, and a Documentation of Performance is submitted for evaluation by a faculty panel.

Two examples of contracts from the Human Resource Management and Leadership clusters are reproduced below. Note two features not found in other contracts in this book: feedback plans and anticipated obstacles.

This selection was submitted by Harry F. Evarts, group vice-president, research and development, American Management Association.

Of special interest:

□ The use of a generic model of competencies for managers as a tool for diagnosis of needs for learning and formulation of objectives.
□ Emphasis on performance assessment for admission and graduation.
□ Use of the workplace as a primary resource for learning and application of learnings.
□ Provision for systematic feedback.

AMA Competency-Development Plan

Student:
Cluster: Human Resource Management
Competency: Accurate self-assessment
Goal: To seek help to improve on soliciting and accepting criticism

	Actions	Target Dates for Completion
Educating myself about the competency	Read *Managing Self-Esteem in Organizations.*	3/25
Practice and application of the competency	1. Meet with my former superior, with whom there has been an undercurrent of attempts to get past the barriers I have erected. Request his assessment and his help, including honest criticism.	
	2. Meet with my present superior, who has been through a similar exercise and who seems willing and anxious to practice all the various competencies. Ask for his evaluation of my diagnosis and his help in overcoming my resistance.	3/30
	3. Practice openness through use of Positive Regard indicators with subordinates. Gauge reactions and, when timing is right, request help.	Ongoing
Feedback plans	Document each instance of criticism and follow up with person who gave it (3 months?) to see if he or she perceives any improvement.	Ongoing

I can anticipate the following obstacles:

Personal: My tendency to respond to critical remarks with witty sarcasms will not disappear overnight.

Situation: Past history of being unwilling to accept constructive criticism has made subordinates, superiors, and peers unwilling to come forward with comments.

Sources of help: Personal friends whom I can ask for assistance.

AMA Competency-Development Plan

Student:
Cluster: Leadership
Competency: Self-confidence
Goal: Learn to express less ambivalence about decisions I have made.

	Actions	Target Dates for Completion
Educating myself about the competency	1. Read *When I Say No I Feel Guilty*.	April 1
	2. Note how my boss gives me feedback on this competency.	
Practice and application of the competency	1. Make a major decision within my authority without consulting my peers and particularly my boss.	April 15
	2. Do this several times this month without asking for feedback.	Ongoing
	3. Make positive comments about decisions I have made recently.	Ongoing
	4. Make a point to make decisions about my children before my wife does.	Ongoing
Feedback plans	1. Ask subordinates for feedback.	June 1
	2. Ask my wife for feedback.	June 1

I can anticipate the following obstacles:

Personal: Being able to accept negative comments by my peers on decisions I have made.
Situation: None.
Sources of help: Subordinates and peers.
My wife.

Observations and Reflections

One of the problems almost universally encountered in continuing professional development programs is the inaccessibility, in many
instances, of resources for learning. The University of Southern
California program attacks that problem by providing learners with the
services of an educational specialist, an information brokering service
located in a medical library, and a peer-support group. Gordon
College's approach is to provide small grants to enable the learners to
buy the necessary learning resources. The program of the American
Management Association delegates primary responsibility for providing
needed resources to the learners' work sites. I have no evidence that
any of these approaches is superior to the others; each one seems to me
to be a creative solution uniquely adapted to the conditions in each
situation. All three programs demonstrate the utilization of one of the
most underused resources available to all of us—the resources of our
peers.

The formats of the learning contracts in the three programs are all
different, but all three—using different terminology—call for specification of learning objectives, strategies and resources for accomplishing
the objectives, and evaluation of the accomplishment of the objectives.
I found the addition in the American Management Association's
program of the specification of feedback plans and anticipated obstacles
to be especially useful.

EIGHT

Degree Programs

■ As colleges and universities began experiencing a shrinkage of the traditional college-age population in the late 1960s and 1970s, they looked to the population of working and homemaking adults to fill the tuition void (Vermilye, 1972, 1974). But most of these adults could not attend classes on campus full-time, and so there was a rapid expansion of nontraditional (evening and weekend) and external (off-campus study) degree programs (Houle, 1973; Sullivan, 1983). In order for the learners to have a coherent and systematic plan of study, the practice of having students contract for total degree programs came into increasing use. Usually the degree contract is negotiated between a student and a faculty committee and is monitored by a mentor or coordinator.

This chapter presents four selections that describe different procedures used in developing contracts and provides examples of degree contracts. The first example is a contract for a Ph.D. degree in human development at the Fielding Institute, headquartered in Santa Barbara, California. This program has no residence requirement (except for a five-day "Admissions and Contract Workshop") and offers no courses (but does offer occasional optional workshops and seminars around the country). Each student chooses a mentor, a program director (a full-time staff member), and a doctoral committee. Degree requirements are met by the learner's "assessing" in four required knowledge areas and four additional knowledge areas elected by the learner from nine options and by writing a dissertation.

The second example is a contract for a bachelor of arts degree at Metropolitan State University, St. Paul, Minnesota. Entering learners must have completed two years of undergraduate work at other institutions and attend a ten-week "Individualized Educational Planning" course. The degree contract is negotiated with a contracting committee and shows how an appropriate level of competency will be achieved and demonstrated in five competency areas. For each competency a learning assessment agreement is drafted by the learner

197

and reviewed by an assessment office. The degree is awarded when all assessments have been successfully completed.

The third example is a contract for a bachelor of liberal studies degree at the College of Liberal Studies, University of Oklahoma. The program includes core studies in the humanities, natural sciences, and social sciences and additional studies through learning contracts that are geared to each learner's personal needs and interests. Learning Contract Agreements are prepared by learners with the help of a contract adviser and are reviewed by a committee of the college.

The fourth example is a "study plan" for a Ph.D. degree in organizational behavior and development at George Washington University, Washington, D.C. It is not a "contract" in the same sense as the preceding examples, in that the principal learning resources are campus-based courses. But it does permit learners to plan the sequence of their courses and to specify how each will contribute to their long-range goals. And it does allow freedom for the learners to specify supplemental learning strategies, such as independent study, field experiences, workshops, and conferences. The learner who submitted this example tells me that the effect it had on her was to make her courses seem much more relevant to her goals and to put them into the context of a more sequential developmental process than she had experienced in previous course programs.

■ SELECTION 20

Contracting for a Ph.D. Degree in Human Development at the Fielding Institute

☐ The Fielding Institute is a fully accredited institution of higher education, headquartered in Santa Barbara, California, that offers two programs leading to master's and doctor's degrees in psychology and in human and organizational development (formerly titled "human development"). This selection is by a student in the latter program for whom I was the mentor. Sadly, he died before completing the contract. It is one of the most thoughtful and best-organized degree contracts I have ever received, and I include it both as a superior example and as a memorial to John Hulbert.

Students start the Fielding degree process by attending a five-day Admissions and Contract Workshop, which is held three times a year; this is the only residence requirement. In this workshop they are oriented to the Fielding process, engage in self-diagnostic experiences to determine learning needs, and begin developing their degree contracts with a mentor, a program director (who is a full-time staff member), and a fellow student. The contract must include the core curriculum of four required knowledge areas plus two additional knowledge areas for master's degree students or four additional knowledge areas (elected by the student from nine options) for doctoral students. The contracts specify learning objectives for these academic areas and for the development of human and professional competencies.

For each knowledge area the student chooses a faculty assessor and negotiates an assessment contract with that person. Each assessment in each knowledge area consists of three components: a general overview of the area, a specific aspect for in-depth study, and a practical application project. When all eight knowledge areas and a dissertation have been completed, the student completes a comprehensive written assessment and a final oral review.

In this selection I have included the summary sheet of the degree contract, two knowledge-area assessment contracts (out of the eight), and the projected time schedule.

Of special interest:

□ Specification of eight "knowledge areas" to be included in the Ph.D. program.
□ A narrative statement of career goals and the relevance of this program to them.
□ An assessment contract in research.
□ An assessment contract in Human Experience and Behavior.
□ A projected schedule for completing the degree requirements.

The Fielding Institute
Study Contract

John R. Hulbert
student's name

907-479-6536
phone number

POB 80866
address

Fairbanks, Alaska 99708
city, state, zip

2/4/81
date submitted

Dr. Malcolm Knowles
mentor

Ph.D.—Human Development
degree sought

Adult & Continuing Education
emphasis

STUDY AREAS	ASSESSORS
1. Research	Dr. Renata Tesch
2. Concepts of Human Development	Dr. Denise Brielby
3. Professional Specialty	Dr. Barbara Mink
4. Theories of Personality	Dr. John Gladfelter
5. Social Psychology	Dr. Don Bushnell
6. Human Experience & Behavior	Dr. Malcolm Knowles
7. Current Policy & Hum. Rights Iss.	Dr. Malcolm Knowles
8. Change Issues & the Future	Dr. Will McWhinney

CONTRACT APPROVED

student

mentor

program director

Research Committee:

chairperson   student

external examiner

I.   INTRODUCTION

Learner: John Hulbert   Program: Ph.D., Human Development (Adult & Cont.
                                                                              Ed.)
Mentor: Dr. Malcolm Knowles
Program Director: Dr. Renata Tesch   Date: January 30, 1981

NARRATIVE	COMMENTS

1. My overall career goal at this time is to develop and successfully operate a profit-oriented international OD/HRD training and consulting business organization which will serve the Pacific Rim area.

2. This goal developed over the course of the past three years during which time I was instrumental in developing a regional adult education service organization in Interior Alaska. Services are provided through a nonprofit corporation holding approximately $1.2 million in grants and contracts. As a result of experiences gained through the development and operation of this program, I became involved in staff and organizational development activities (for my own organization as well as others). In order to keep finding myself in situations that provide adequate opportunities for personal and professional growth, it seemed logical that developing a profit-oriented OD/HRD training and consulting organization was the next step in my career. In addition to a desire to increase my income, it also seemed to me that operating in the profit sector would give me (1) freer rein in the development and operation of programs than is possible through a nonprofit, (2) a clearer picture of my strengths and abilities, and (3) a greater chance to test myself (since the success of a nonprofit is not always a true measure of competence in the human services) as well as a greater chance to learn more concerning staff and organizational development (and at a faster rate) than might be possible in any other manner at this time.

II. ACADEMIC STUDY AREAS: #1—RESEARCH

Learner: John Hulbert   Program: Ph.D., Human Development (Adult & Cont.
                                                              Ed.)
Mentor: Dr. Malcolm Knowles
Program Director: Dr. Renata Tesch   Date: January 30, 1981
Assessor/Consultant: Dr. Renata Tesch

OVERVIEW   COMMENTS

1. OVERVIEW

   A. Learning Objective

      Become familiar with varieties of research methodology and terminology.

   B. Learning Activities

      1. Carry out a program of readings (to include but not be limited to):

         Evaluating Research Proposals in the Behavioral Sciences; Davitz & Davitz

         How to Calculate Statistics; Fitz-Gibbon & Morris

         The Conduct of Inquiry; Kaplan

         The Research Act; Golden

         Phenomenological & Transformative Research; Tesch

         Appraising Educational Research; Millman & Gowin

         A Manual for Writers; Turabian

         Qualitative Evaluation Methods; Patton

         Evaluating Action Programs; Weiss

         Educational Evaluation; Popham

         Hip Pocket Guide to Planning & Evaluation; Craig

         Questionnaires: Design & Use; Berdie & Anderson

      2. Develop a questionnaire related to the research competencies listed in the
         Research area of the Study Guide.

3. Interview 5–10 individuals involved in various aspects of research connected with the University of Alaska and other institutions using the abovementioned questionnaire.

4. Discuss the development of a research project (formulation of research question, research design, etc.) with 5–10 individuals who are working on or have completed a doctoral thesis.

5. Maintain contact (by phone and/or letter) with Renata Tesch regarding problems encountered, resources sought, etc., during the course of the study.

C. Assessment

1. Provide assessor with an audiocassette on which I discuss a number of topics mentioned in the competency list in the Research area of the Study Guide.

2. Respond to any questions assessor might have relating to my comments on the first cassette with a second cassette.

2. IN-DEPTH TOPIC

A. Learning Objective

Demonstrate an understanding of the philosophical foundations of research and an awareness of a number of problems regarding the nature of research (its limitations, etc.) that a philosophical analysis of the field might raise.

B. Learning Activities

1. See readings: 1.B.1.
2. Locate additional readings in the philosophy of research.

3. Carry out a series of discussions with members of the Philosophy Department of the University of Alaska, Fairbanks, regarding questions raised by my readings.

C. Assessment

   1. Write and submit a short paper to assessor (5–15 pages) discussing and analyzing one particular aspect of the philosophical foundations of research.

3. APPLICATION

A. Learning Objective

   Demonstrate the ability to apply research methodology and terminology by developing and having accepted a Ph.D. research project proposal.

B. Learning Activities

   1. Develop an acceptable research project proposal: determine research question, approach, outline, etc.

C. Assessment

   1. Submit a research proposal to appropriate Fielding faculty; revise as necessary until proposal is accepted.

II. ACADEMIC STUDY AREAS: #6—Human Experience & Behavior

Learner: John Hulbert
Mentor: Dr. Malcolm Knowles
Program Director: Dr. Renata Tesch
Assessor/Consultant: Dr. Malcolm Knowles

Program: Ph.D., Human Development (Adult & Cont. Ed.)
Date: January 30, 1981

1. OVERVIEW

A. Learning Objective

Demonstrate an understanding of the works of the following major learning theorists (Tolman, Skinner, Watson, Thorndike, Pavlov, Gagné, Ausubel, Bruner, Piaget, Brown, Maslow, and Rogers) in terms of (1) how each relates to the behaviorist, cognitive, and humanistic viewpoint, (2) how the work of each is applicable in terms of the learner's level of learning ability and the level of complexity of the learning task, (3) the impact of each upon current learning systems for youth and adults, and (4) the strengths and weaknesses of each in terms of having developed a holistic point of view of human development.

B. Learning Activities

1. Develop and carry out a program of readings of primary and secondary source materials related to the works of major learning theorists.

2. Develop an annotated bibliography of works made use of during the course of the study for potential use by other Fielding students.

3. Carry out a series of interviews regarding learning theory with members of the University of Alaska Departments of Education and Philosophy.

C. Assessment

1. Provide assessor with copy of annotated bibliography.

2. Write and submit a 10–20 page paper analyzing the differences and similarities between two or more major theorists.

2. IN-DEPTH TOPIC

A. Learning Objective

Demonstrate a thorough understanding of the theory and practice of andragogy; specifically, its historical roots and development, its relationship to the pedagogical model, its potential usefulness in a variety of personal and social settings, and its current application in the fields of business and education.

B. Learning Activities

1. Develop and carry out a study of learning resources produced by (or participated in by) Malcolm Knowles.

2. Maintain contact with members of the Andragogy Network.

3. Develop (as a follow-up to the 1980 ALPA Summer Institute on Linking the Worlds of Education and Work, facilitated by Malcolm Knowles) an Alaska Learning Network, a network of individuals interested in applying the andragogical model to their particular fields.

4. Maintain a record of the growth and activities of the Alaska Learning Network.

C. Assessment

1. Carry out one or more public presentations to professional groups, applying the andragogical model to the presentation.

2. Provide assessor with written analysis of the presentations.

3. During an assessment session with the assessor, answer questions regarding the learning objective.

3. APPLICATION

A. Learning Objective

Demonstrate the ability to apply the andragogical model to the learning processes of youth.

B. Learning Activities

1. Work with my own children in developing learning plans for their various activities over a period of 9–12 months.

2. Maintain a journal of activities carried out with my children during this period in terms of: their response to the concept of planning personal learning and other activities, their developing abilities in regard to self-assessment and evaluation, effects of this work upon their overall motivation to learn, etc.

3. Work as closely as possible with the children's schoolteachers during this period.

4. Contact Allen Tough (and others) to find out what additional resources might be available in this area.

C. Assessment

1. Prepare an article for publication regarding the project and submit a copy to assessor (as well as sending one to the publication).

2. Discuss project with children's teachers at the project's conclusion to see what effect, if any, their work at home has had upon their work in school.

3. Discuss findings of the project with assessor and answer any questions arising from the discussion. Also, plan for long-term extension of the project in some form.

VI. TIMETABLE

Learner: John Hulbert
Mentor: Dr. Malcolm Knowles
Program Director: Dr. Renata Tesch

Program: Ph.D., Human Development (Adult & Cont. Ed.)
Date: January 30, 1981

AREA	1980	1981	1982
	J J A S O N D	J F M A M J J A S O N D	J F M A M J

#1: RESEARCH

#2: CONCEPTS OF HUMAN DEVELOPMENT

#3.: PROFESSIONAL SPECIALTY: CONSULTING

#4: THEORIES OF PERSONALITY

#5: SOCIAL PSYCHOLOGY

#6: HUMAN EXPERIENCE & BEHAVIOR

#7: CURRENT POLICY & HUMAN RIGHTS ISSUES

#8: CHANGE ISSUES & THE FUTURE

RESEARCH PROJECT

■ SELECTION 21

Contracting for a B.A. Degree at Metropolitan State University

□ Metropolitan State University (formerly Minnesota Metropolitan State College), in St. Paul, was established in 1971 to serve adult students not otherwise being reached by existing higher education institutions. It emphasizes the use of community resources, including the holding of classes in underutilized facilities of schools, libraries, museums, churches, parks, and commercial institutions and the employment of part-time faculty members whose major employment is in community organizations, agencies, and businesses. It has a core of full-time faculty members and administrators, but there are about ten times as many "community faculty members."

Entering students must have completed two years of satisfactory work at another college or university or be able to demonstrate an equivalent amount of education by other means. On admission (at any time of the year), they receive an Individualized Educational Planning (IEP) text and participate in a ten-week IEP course, the objectives of both of which are:

1. To acquaint students with Metro U's educational philosophy and methods.
2. To aid students in examining, clarifying, and defining their individualized educational goals.
3. To examine thoroughly the question "What is an educated person?"
4. To assist students in understanding the links between liberal learning and career success.
5. To investigate the use of prior experiential learning to meet educational goals.
6. To introduce students to the resources and personnel of the Metro U learning network.
7. To guide students in writing appropriate individualized degree plans.

8. To give students a working knowledge of community resources.
9. To prepare students for lifelong learning activities.
10. To ready students for primary responsibility and authority over the content and direction of their education [IEP text, p. 5].

The student is assigned to a permanent faculty adviser and a special assessment, advising, and contracting committee to work with the student in developing a degree contract. This contract is examined by a contract review committee, made up of faculty and students, which may require revisions before acceptance.

The degree contract shows how an appropriate level of competence is to be achieved and demonstrated in each of the five competence areas that the university has defined as essential: (1) vocation, (2) communication, (3) community, (4) culture, science, and tradition, and (5) avocation. For each competence, the learner drafts a learning assessment agreement that describes the competence, specifies the process by which it will be achieved, proposes how it will be evaluated, and nominates an evaluator. These agreements are reviewed by an assessment office.

This selection includes an educational goals statement by a typical student, a transcripted credit chart, a degree plan table of contents, and three examples of learning assessment agreements. This selection was provided by Jan M. Byrne, director, institutional research, Metropolitan State University.

Of special interest:

□ Educational goals statement.
□ Degree plan.
□ Learning assessment agreements.

Metropolitan State University Degree Plan
Educational Goals Statement

In the space below (and using any additional pages as necessary), please write a statement of your educational goals. This statement should: (1) summarize your views on the question: What is an educated person?; (2) detail your past learning experiences, both formal and experiential; (3) present a general outline of your career goals; and (4) outline how you will address the five competence areas (communication; community; culture, science, and tradition; vocation; and avocation) through competencies selected for your degree plan.

I want to develop a career in management. Currently, I am employed with a local corporation that specializes in computer systems. I work in the accounting section for international sales. Several training programs are available in my company for entry-level managers; however, a college degree is necessary to qualify.

My response to the question, what is an educated person? is influenced by my previous education and the experiences I have gained in my career. I agree with Pelligrino's point that having a degree doesn't guarantee that one is an educated person. I've seen several contradictions in professional settings to a direct equation between a college degree and an educated person. An educated person must blend theory with practice, must learn from mistaken assumptions, and must make a commitment to learning throughout a lifetime of experience and study. My work in the computer field also convinces me that the educated person of the next decade must blend traditional liberal learning with a knowledge of the computer. This knowledge, however, cannot be solely technical. It must include a keen understanding of the social, ethical, and political effects of computer revolution. I have identified several essential areas of liberal learning that will sophisticate my life and career experiences. These include work in history, philosophy, and languages. I expect that my personal conception of what makes an educated person will also motivate me to carefully evaluate theories and knowledge gained in one discipline with another (such as ethics and organizational theories, or history and literary analysis).

My previous education encompasses two years at the community college where I received an A.S. degree. Much of my course work is related to accounting. I completed the minimum in terms of "general education" requirements.

In addition to my formal education, I have had significant learning experiences outside the structure of formal classroom study. I plan to include some of this learning in my degree plan as it relates to my career goals and general education goals. Specifically, I will develop prior learning competencies in community organizing, religion, literary analysis, and recruiting, interviewing, and selecting.

In the career or "vocation" area of competence, I will need to concentrate on specific courses offered at Metro U that will cover the basic theoretical foundations of a management career. Although the training program in my company will cover much of my training, I want an overall theoretical framework to measure the training program. In addition, I will concentrate on the field of marketing as an entry-level specialty. This will be combined with my previous work in accounting.

In the other areas of competence, I have two objectives: (1) to pursue liberal learning opportunities that will enhance understandings, skills, and qualities I need to become a successful, effective manager and (2) to develop some lifelong learning interests apart from my career concerns (as a possible antidote to workplace pressures). I want to use independent study and internships as learning strategies to accomplish these objectives.

Transcripted Credit Chart

Using a duplicate copy of your transcripts, list your transfer credits
and courses accepted for admission by Metro U under the
appropriate general competence areas.

Communication

English 121, 122, 123
Speech
Business Communication

Community

Economics
Public Health
Sociology

Vocation

Financial Accounting I-III
Managerial Accounting I-II
Cost Accounting I-II
Intro to Computers
COBOL
Accounting Internship
Federal and State Income Tax
Business Decision
Intro to Business
Business Law
Small Business Management
Sales

Culture, Science, and Tradition

Art History
Biology
Mathematics
Psychology

Avocation

Winter Camping
Cross Country Skiing

Degree Plan Table of Contents

General Competence Area	Competence Title (key words/subject area)	Priors	Classes	FDIS	SDIS	Internship	Other Inst.	Amendments	Completed
1. Vocation	Statistics		X						
2. "	Cases in Business Policy		X						
3. "	Organizational Management		X						
4. "	Managerial Finance		X						
5. "	Managerial Aspects of Data Processing		X						
6. "	American Political Process			X					
7. "	Marketing Principles		X						
8. "	Marketing: Government Regulation		X						
9. "	Marketing Research			X					
10. "	Recruiting, Interviewing, and Selecting	X							
11. Communication	IEP		X						
12. "	Communication Patterns and Breakdowns		X						
13. "	Language Variations				X				
14. "	Spanish I and II		X						
15. Community	Community Organizing	X							
16. "	Religious Faiths	X							
17. "	Internship: Family Services					X			
18. C.S.T.	Literary Analysis	X							
19. "	Logic		X						
20. "	Views of Human Nature		X						
21. "	Historian as Investigator		X						
22. "	Prejudice in American Culture			X					
23. Avocation	Minnesota Mammals		X						
24. "	Internship: Children's Theatre					X			

Note: The abbreviations used above have the following meanings: FDIS, faculty-directed independent study; SDIS, student-directed independent study; C.S.T., culture, science, and tradition.

Competence Description

competence # _____13_____

Competence Statement: Knows the history, concepts, and methodology of modern linguistics and their relevance to areas of social and personal concern and can apply in evaluating popular notions about language.

Achieved By:

___ Prior Life/Work Experience
___ Internship
___ Community-Based Learning

___ Classroom Learning
xx Independent Study
___ Other

Process Description: Student-designed independent study; readings from texts and supplementary materials; research project on language variations within urban subcultures.

Suggested Measurement Techniques:

___ Oral Interview
___ Objective Test
xx Product Evaluation
___ Simulation Exercise

___ Performance Test
___ Essay Exam
___ Situational Observation

Description of Measurement Techniques (if necessary): Product evaluation of research project and other exercises

---

Evaluator(s):

Name and Qualifications of Evaluator(s):
1. (Metro U Evaluator)
   Miriam Meyers, Metro U associate professor
2.

Competence Description

competence #   15

Competence Statement: Knows the concepts and methods of community organizing well enough to bring about the establishment of a new community agency for children.

Achieved By:

xx Prior Life/Work   ___ Classroom
    Experience   Learning
___ Internship   ___ Independent
___ Community-Based   Study
    Learning   ___ Other

Process Description: From 1973 to 1975 I was involved in organizing a community volunteer group devoted to establishing a children's recreation and art center. I worked with a number of professional consultants to establish legal and administrative aspects for the center. I read and held extensive interviews with experts concerning the problems of community organizing and working with local government. I held meetings, organized research, presented written proposal to city government, raised funds.

Suggested Measurement Techniques:

xx Oral Interview   ___ Performance
___ Objective Test   Test
xx Product Evaluation   ___ Essay Exam
___ Simulation   xx Situational
    Exercise   Observation

Description of Measurement Techniques (if necessary):

Evaluator(s):

Name and Qualifications of Evaluator(s):
1. (Metro U Evaluator)
   Carol Ryan, Metro U advising staff associate
2. Robert V. Browning, attorney, St. Paul, Minnesota; adviser to community groups, lobbyist; member of Governor's Council on Children's Agencies

Competence Description

competence # _____18_____

Competence Statement: Knows concepts and techniques of literary analysis well enough to analyze and compare selected twentieth-century novels in relation to their style, structure, and thematic development.

Achieved By:

XX_ Prior Life/Work   ___ Classroom
       Experience   Learning
___ Internship   ___ Independent
___ Community-Based   Study
       Learning   ___ Other

Process Description: For the past 10 years I have completed extensive reading related to twentieth-century literature, literary criticism, and literary analysis. (I have prepared a bibliography to accompany my plan.)

Suggested Measurement Techniques:

XX_ Oral Interview   ___ Performance
___ Objective Test   Test
XX_ Product Evaluation   ___ Essay Exam
___ Simulation   ___ Situational
       Exercise   Observation

Description of Measurement Techniques (if necessary): Oral interview on readings; research report on selected authors

---

Evaluator(s):

Name and Qualifications of Evaluator(s):
1.   (Metro U Evaluator)
       Carol Holmberg, Metro U professor
2.

■ SELECTION 22

Contracting for a Bachelor of Liberal Studies Degree at the College of Liberal Studies, University of Oklahoma

□ One of the pioneering institutions in the development of special degree programs for adults, the University of Oklahoma established the College of Continuing Education in 1960 (renamed the College of Liberal Studies in 1970) to serve part-time adult students.

This selection includes the "Guide to the Bachelor of Liberal Studies," which explains the process of contracting for a total degree program to entering students, and three examples of contracts for units of the core areas of the humanities, natural sciences, and social sciences. This selection was provided by Daniel A. Davis, associate dean, College of Liberal Studies.

Of special interest:

□ The contract learning agreement.
□ Components of a learning contract.
□ Strategies for a learning contract.
□ Preparing the contract proposal.
□ Approval of the contract.
□ Completion of the contract.

Guide to the Bachelor of Liberal Studies
College of Liberal Studies
University of Oklahoma

Contract Learning Agreement

The Contract Learning Agreement feature of the B.L.S. program was designed to let you take an active part in the development of your total study program. Your B.L.S. curriculum will include core material in the humanities, the natural sciences, and the social sciences and additional studies through learning contracts which are attuned to your personal needs and interest. The contract studies are to be closely associated with core study and should reflect your career interest or relate to a personal or topical interest.

Here are some examples of the types of study programs which can be accommodated in the learning contract concept. *Alice* has been an active participant in community service groups for many years; she particularly enjoys working several hours each week in a senior citizens center. She thinks that through contract studies in the B.L.S. program she could gain knowledge which will relate to her experience and help her improve her service. *Larry* has had great success in the engineering firm where he works, and he is slated to move into a position which is concerned with environmental issues involved in the company's proposals and designs. He anticipates that the B.L.S. core studies will provide a broader base of knowledge in the humanities, social sciences, and natural sciences and that the individualized contract learning will deal with environmental issues related to each of the areas. *Mary Sue* always has been fascinated with the history of the American West, and she is proud of the fact that her great-grandfather was with the original Oregon Trail group. The contract studies associated with Mary's B.L.S. core areas will provide her greater understanding about the literature, history, social background, education, health, and other circumstances of the people who developed the American West.

You will receive Learning Contract Proposal information after you have enrolled in each area of independent study. The college staff will review the general nature of the contract before referring it to a faculty member with the appropriate background and expertise to assist you.

The faculty member will receive your proposal and outline the activities and studies you are to pursue in fulfilling the objectives. Likewise, the professor will describe the means by which your performance on the contract will be evaluated.

Components of a Learning Contract

From your Learning Contract Proposal, then, your adviser will develop a Contract Learning Agreement reflecting the following:

1. Statement of the general purpose of the study;
2. Statement of the specific purpose of the contract;
3. Indication of the relationship of the contract study to the core area study;
4. Outline of the learning activities; and
5. Evaluative techniques to be used.

Strategies for a Learning Contract

There are several learning strategies which would be appropriate for the Learning Contract, and you should explore the various ways in which your studies could be designed. While content of the contract will be based on problems, issues, or ideas you wish to study, the important thing to remember is that study should relate to the corresponding core area as well. Some of the learning strategies you might use are:

1. Directed reading—books, articles, journals, or other materials outlined by the faculty adviser or negotiated between you and the adviser.
2. Special study units—several special study units have been developed by the College of Liberal Studies or are associated with special alternatives such as the Open Learning Fire

Service Program or the Legal Assistant Program. Information about special study units will be provided for each study area.

3. Internship—a work or service experience may be carried out under supervision. The contract adviser will work with you in the development of the conditions of the internship.

4. Formal courses from academic institutions—courses from accredited colleges and universities may fulfill a contract agreement. The course must be for at least two hours' credit and be at the upper-division level; you must make a grade of C or better to establish credit. If these and related criteria outlined in the Advanced Standing section of this *Guide* are met, a previously completed course may stand for a contract learning activity.

5. Courses from nonacademic institutions—nonacademic courses completed through business, government, community, or other organizations—can be considered for contract learning activities. These courses are subject to assessment of their purposes, the learning activities including the level of the content, the means of evaluation employed, and the relevance of the course to the B.L.S. study area. You will need to provide documentation of your involvement and the extent of your learning.

6. Field experiences, observations, projects—these and other possible activities could become a learning contract. Included could be such things as in-service vocational training, community or personal experience, travel, or independent research. These activities are subject to criteria development, content evaluation, assessment of learning achieved, and the relevance of the learning to the B.L.S. area.

You may vary the learning strategy used to complete the contracts with the three core areas. For example, you might complete readings in the humanities phase, do a field experience in social sciences, and combine readings and a project for the natural sciences. You will have a contract adviser in each area and will develop the contract with his or her guidance.

Preparing the Contract Learning Agreement

After you have enrolled in an area and have received your initial core study materials, you will receive specific information about contract possibilities in that area. A Learning Contract Proposal form will be provided; you are to complete it and return it to the College Office.

Approval of the Contract Learning Agreement

Each of your Contract Learning Proposals will be reviewed by a committee in the college, and both you and the contract adviser will receive a copy of the approved Contract Learning Agreement.

Completion of the Contract

The means by which you are to accomplish the learning contract goals will be written into the contract agreement. You will provide evidence of your accomplishment to your adviser, who will evaluate your work and ultimately notify the College Office that the contract has been fulfilled.

You may complete a contract after finishing the core reading assignments in an area or concurrently with your core readings. The former order would help you see a greater relationship between the core content and your individualized contract study; however, by carefully planning your contract with your adviser, you should be able to begin the work at any time.

B.L.S. Contract Learning Agreement

Student _____ Study Area Humanities_____
Adviser _ C. Beesley_____

A. Student's General Purpose:

To investigate and experiment in the making of natural dyes from indigenous Oklahoma plants.

B. Specific Purposes of This Contract:

To experiment in the making of natural dyes and then use them to actually tint natural fibers. The student will identify the botanical plant, formulate a recipe for the dye, dye the fiber. She will then weave the dyed fibers into cloth.

C. Relation of the Contract to the Core Area Study:

Betty will be consulting old Indian recipes, visiting the Seminole Nation museum to look at the historic tradition of clothing dyeing as well as the designs of the artifacts. This along with the collecting of plants and the dyemaking process will involve a number of integrated areas.

D. Learning Activities (may involve more than one type):

1. Types: __ Directed Reading __ Nonacademic Institution Course
__ Traditional Course _X_ Special Study Unit _X_ Project/ Internship
2. Specific Activities (reading list; unit title; course title; project outline; or other descriptive information):

She will submit a bibliography, describe her activities, and include in her paper samples of the plants, the dyed swatches, and possibly some handwoven samples.

E. Evaluation (full description of means of determining whether the purpose of the learning agreement has been accomplished):

Evaluation will be based on the paper and on the samples.

F.   Learning Agreement Approval:

Student _____ Adviser _____

Review Committee: CLS _____

Area Faculty _____

Date _____

B.L.S. Contract Learning Agreement

Student _____ Study Area Social Sciences _____
Adviser R. E. Hilbert ____

A. Student's General Purpose:

To better understand the structure of kinship systems in human societies.

B. Specific Purposes of This Contract:

To study the historical development of the Scottish clan as a type of kinship system.

C. Relation of the Contract to the Core Area Study:

A study of kinship systems falls clearly within the subject area of the social sciences with its emphasis on social organization.

D. Learning Activities (may involve more than one type):

1. Types: X Directed Reading/Paper __ Nonacademic Institution Course
    __ Traditional Course __ CLS Study Unit __ Project/ Internship
2. Specific Activities (reading list; unit title; course title; project outline; or other descriptive information):

The student will (1) consult the following books and then (2) write a paper on the subject being investigated.

TITLE	AUTHOR
The Story of Civilization (12 volumes)	Will Durant
Clans and Chiefs	Ian Grimble
History of England	Lord Macaulay
Scots Kith and Kin	
Scottish Roots	Alwyn James
The Scottish Tartans	
The Romantic Scotland	Kenneth McKellar
Various maps and guidebooks	

E. Evaluation (full description of means of determining whether the purposes of the learning agreement have been accomplished):

Performance on the project will be evaluated by reference to the paper which is to be submitted and to any conversations on that paper which might develop in the course of its preparation.

F. Learning Agreement Approval:

Student _____ Adviser _____

Review Committee: CLS _____

Area Faculty _____

Date _____

B.L.S. Contract Learning Agreement

Student _____ Study Area __Natural Sciences_____

Adviser _John Lancaster___

A. Student's General Purpose:

Increase knowledge of coral reef biology.

B. Specific Purposes of This Contract:

To study the biota of a coral reef associated with Ponape Island, Eastern Caroline Islands, Micronesia.

C. Relation of the Contract to the Core Area Study:

Represents an in-depth study of a facet of biology.

D. Learning Activities (may involve more than one type):

 1. Types: __ Directed Reading _x_ Nonacademic Institution Course
 __ Traditional Course __ CLS Study Unit __ Project/ Internship
 2. Specific Activities (reading list; unit title; course title; project outline; or other descriptive information):

 1. Visit Ponape Island.
 2. Photograph and catalogue the biological features of its coral reef.
 3. Present the material in the form of a photo album and related cassette tape describing the observations.

E. Evaluation (full description of means of determining whether the purposes of the learning agreement have been accomplished):

Results will be compiled as a photographic record detailed with a cassette tape. The tape and photographs will be reviewed as a basis for evaluation.

F.   Learning Agreement Approval:

Student _____ Adviser __John Lancaster__

Review Committee: CLS _____

Area Faculty _____

Date _____

■ SELECTION 23

Study Plan for a Ph.D. Degree in Organizational Behavior and Development at George Washington University

☐ The School of Government and Business at George Washington University gives entering Ph.D. candidates one year in which to develop a study plan for the entire degree program. In consultation with a major adviser and a supporting field adviser, along with other faculty members and students, the candidate completes the study plan form, which, when approved, becomes the "contract" for the degree. This selection, submitted by doctoral student Kathy L. Kaplan on the suggestion of her major adviser, Jerry Harvey, shows how she will accomplish the degree requirements through courses and a variety of other activities.

Of special interest:

☐   Summary statement of study plan requirements.
☐   Other activities.
☐   Evaluation processes.
☐   Long-range goals.
☐   Basic preparation.
☐   Analytical methods.
☐   Proposed activities: (1) major field, (2) supporting field.
☐   Relationship between goals and activities.

Doctoral Candidate Study Plan
Committee on Doctoral Studies
School of Government and Business Administration
The George Washington University
Washington, D.C. 20052

Summary Statement of Study Plan Requirements

NAME   Kathy L. Kaplan

Dept.	No.	Course Descriptive Title	Type of Grade
Mgt.	390	Philosophical Foundations of Administrative Research	Credit
Mgt.	311–312	Public-Private Sector Institutions and Relationships	Credit
Mgt.	701	Ethical, Moral, and Spiritual Issues of Management	Grade
Educ.	180	Computer Literacy	Credit
Acct.	201	Financial Accounting	Credit
Mgt.	205	Organization and Management— doctoral credit	Grade
Mgt.	215	Conflict Management	Grade
PAd.	296	Statistical Application in Public Admin.	Grade
BAd.	246	Product/Service Marketing	Credit
Mgt.	216	Cross-Cultural Management	Audit
Soc.	241	Sociology of Work and Organizations	Credit
Mgt.	398a	Advanced Reading and Research with Jerry Harvey on Unconscious Factors in Organizations	Credit
PAd.	221	Organizational Theory and the Public Sector	Credit
PAd.	373	Public Administration and American Political and Social Institutions	Credit
Educ.	282	Introduction to Qualitative Research Methods	Grade
Mgt.	398b	Advanced Reading and Research with Peter Vaill on History of OD and Major Concepts/Theories	Credit
PAd.	261	Policy Analysis in Public Administration	Credit
PAd.	264	Public Program Evaluation	Grade
Mgt.	398c	Advanced Reading and Research with Jerry Harvey on Learning, Creativity, and Evaluating Effectiveness	Credit

PAd.	374	Trends in Public Administration Theory	Grade
PAd.	377	Social Action and Public Policy	Grade
Mgt.	391	Methodological Foundations of Administrative Research	Credit

---

Kathy L. Kaplan

Degree: DPA

Undergraduate degree: B.S.

Institution: University of Wisconsin, Madison, Wisconsin

Major: Occupational Therapy

Year: 1972

March 9, 1985

Full Time

Graduate Degree: M.S.

Institution: Virginia Commonwealth University, Richmond, Virginia

Major: Occupational Therapy

Year: 1983

Major Field of Study:
   Organizational Behavior and
   Development

Supporting Field of Study:
   Public Administration

Adviser: Jerry Harvey

Adviser: Steve Chitwood

Long-Range Goals

My previous educational and work experiences have shown me that I thrive when involved in related projects which I find interesting, challenging, and varied. I never could have predicted that I would be seeking a doctorate in organizational behavior and development because, though I usually know my general direction, my clarity about specific meaningful activities tends to evolve. While I am clear about my major goals over the next five years, I am sure the plan will have minor changes and develop further as I learn from each of the experiences. I know that I feel fully engaged when writing, applying theory to practice, and learning with others. Therefore, I want to develop the skills, knowledge, and self-awareness which will allow me to creatively, critically, and competently contribute to my chosen fields. I want to:

1.   Be a university professor at a good-quality institution:

      to teach doctoral and master's degree students;

      to participate in associated faculty roles and responsibilities;

      to develop and teach courses related to primary interests.

Content areas I seek to explore include (in no particular order):

      underlying philosophy of professional fields;

      theory development;

      communication and group relations;

      organizational behavior and intervention;

      public policy and private sector relations;

      management and leadership;

      creativity, change, and evaluating effectiveness.

2. Be an effective facilitator of learning:

      to understand generic processes of learning;

      to identify specific learning styles and strategies;

      to apply knowledge skillfully in the design and conduct of a variety of learning situations (that is, classroom, workshop, training, consulting, and professional presentation).

3. Be a successful organizational consultant to private, public, and health-oriented organizations in such areas as:

      conflict management and human relations;

      organizing for excellence;

      marketing services;

      program development and program evaluation.

4. Be competent to evaluate, conduct, and supervise social science research:

      to understand the use of quantitative methods;

      to be familiar with using several computer programs;

      to apply qualitative methods in the design of research;

      to analyze and articulate epistemologic and ontologic assumptions.

5. To improve my ability to communicate my ideas through a variety of media:

      to articulate my ideas in conversation clearly, sensitively, persuasively, and authentically;

      to write effectively for various professional purposes and publications, such as administrative, theoretical, anecdotal, or analytical;

to express creatively my ideas using graphic means, such as audiovisuals and photography, as well as verbal means, such as poetry and mythology.

6.   To develop mastery over my "Jablonski." (Jerry Harvey uses this term to convey those areas in which anxiety or other factors threaten integrated self-awareness and self-enhancing action.) Issues for me include:

setting priorities in relation to use of time;

decreasing obsessive and perfectionistic tendencies;

dealing with anger and criticism more easily;

balancing my needs for individuality, connectedness, and intimacy;

trusting and developing my ability to make decisions and think critically;

working on realistic self-assessment and self-regard;

realizing and utilizing personal power;

making an integrated decision about whether to have children.

I
Basic Preparation

My experience in occupational therapy over the past twelve years, as a clinician, educator, consultant, and master's degree student, provided an excellent background for my doctoral-level study in general. Specifically, I find the evaluation–treatment planning–treatment implementation–reevaluation sequence common to clinical practice has great applicability to the problem-solving approaches of consulting relationships and organizational interventions. In addition, master's-level course work in research methods, methods of observation and of data collection, the thesis proposal, and the development of an assessment instrument provided my groundwork in analytical methods. The publication of my master's thesis indicates a capability to design, conduct, and complete a minor research project.

All of my long-range goals reflect a lifelong commitment in which the process of development has already begun. I have published several articles, developed two videotapes, and presented my work at numerous conferences. My teaching appointment at Towson State University demonstrated my interest and capability for facilitating learning. The experience clarified the areas in which I want to teach and the roles and responsibilities of a faculty member. Therefore, additional teaching experience is not a priority in this study plan.

Similarly, my experience developing a system of group treatment for an inpatient psychiatric unit and leading a variety of groups provided me with skills common to the development of workshops and training functions. I also took Mgt. 212, Behavioral Factors in the Process of Change, as part of my master's. My current area of focus is to participate in organized group experiences which will give me feedback on my behavior and allow me to examine managerial and organizational dynamics. I see the development of my use of self and my understanding of the processes and values of the field of organizational behavior and development as key to the fulfillment of my goals.

A primary area I want to develop is my consulting practice. In order to consult competently with both public and private organizations, I believe I need a background in both business and public administration. I want to bring to organizations an understanding of their values and concerns as well as of the political, economic, and social factors impinging on and forming the context for programs, policies, and businesses. I can prepare for such an understanding by developing my basic knowledge of the literature and the theoretical and philosophical foundations of my chosen fields of study.

Proposed Activities

1. Introduction to basic business professional preparation:
   completion of Accounting 201;
   read introductory text on economics;
   read introductory text on marketing.
2. Familiarity with basic public administration preparation:
   read introductory text on public administration.

Evaluation Process

1. Credit (pass/fail); oral evaluation by supporting field adviser (economics is one of major interests); oral evaluation by marketing instructor prior to taking course in service marketing.
2. Oral evaluation by supporting field adviser.

II
Analytical Methods

Proposed Activities

1. Quantitative methods, entailing use of a statistical computer package and applying common statistics to public administration and research: PAd. 296, Statistical Application in Public Administration.
2. Familiarity with computer: Educ. 180, Computer Literacy.
3. Qualitative methods: Educ. 282, Introduction to Qualitative Research Methods.
4. Knowledge about program evaluation: completion of PAd. 264, Public Program Evaluation.
5. Integration of research knowledge in preparation for dissertation proposal: Mgt. 391, Methodological Foundations of Administrative Research.

Evaluation Process

1. Successful completion of course requirements as indicated by course grades.
2. Demonstration of ability to use both quantitative and qualitative analytical methods in actual research projects (small in scale) as evaluated by major and supporting field advisers.

III
Mgt. 390 and 311-312

Required courses were taken fall of 1984 and spring of 1985.

Evaluation Process

Successful completion of course requirements as indicated by course grades.

IV
Major Field: Organizational Behavior and Development

Proposed Activities

1. Fall of 1984, completed independent study with Gordon Lippitt on consultation and conflict management, applying course work to current consulting relationships.
2. Spring of 1985, completed Mgt. 701, Ethical, Moral, and Spiritual Issues of Management, to further expand belief system and methods of expression.
3. Completion of Myers-Briggs Professional Qualifying Program to enhance knowledge about learning styles and preferences. (Will be completed June 1985.)
4. Completion of Mgt. 205 to utilize the case study approach in examining management issues and to include additional readings and discussion with Peter Vaill to add complexity and relevancy of the material commensurate with long-term goals and doctoral-level work. (Include material on organizing for excellence and strategic planning.)
5. Continuation of learning about conflict management in Mgt. 215.
6. Development of a marketing strategy for my consulting services through BAd. 246, Product/Service Marketing.
7. Knowledge of values and differences in other countries: visited India (March 21–April 8, 1985) and to complete Mgt. 216, Cross-Cultural Management.
8. Development of self-awareness, competence, and knowledge about organizational dynamics through participation in at least one group relations conference through A. K. Rice and two through the NTL Institute.
9. Continuation of knowledge about organizations through Soc. 241, Sociology of Work and Organizations.

10. Familiarity with professional issues and people as expressed through their professional conferences. Attendance at at least one professional association meeting in each field, such as the Organizational Development Network, ASPA (American Society of Public Administration), and AOTA (American Occupational Therapy Association).

11. Apprenticeship with experienced consultants and participation in new independent consulting experiences to organizations approximately one to two days per week.

12. Engagement in creative expression of inward journey through poetry, mythology, and graphic means with the aim of greater understanding of unconscious factors affecting organizational life (Mgt. 398a with Jerry Harvey).

13. Integration of knowledge from diverse areas through self-directed readings and dialogue with supervising professor. Advanced readings in Mgt. 398b, the history of major field and critical theoretical contributions; Mgt. 398c, learning, creativity, and evaluating effectiveness.

14. Development of writing and creative capacities and integration of past clinical experience with current learnings about group relations through completion of workbook on groups in occupational therapy. The workbook is a follow-up to a theoretical article submitted for publication last August and accepted for publication with revision in the *American Journal of Occupational Therapy*.

Evaluation Processes

Oral presentation to several professors and students in major field accompanied by written materials in which justification for and description of a course proposal are presented. The course in question will be one which the candidate sees as contributing to the education of SGBA students as well as reflecting the integration of her major theoretical and practical learnings. Rationale for content areas not included in the course will be articulated to demonstrate a wide grasp of the field as well as professional judgment. The type of course, role of the professor, the learning objectives and activities, selected resources, and methods of evaluation will seek to embody the values of the field, authenticity of the candidate, and a critical knowledge of the main issues, underlying assumptions, and limitations of the topic.

V
Supporting Field: Public Administration

1. Development of knowledge about the social, political, and economic factors which impact on management and organizations: completion of PAd. 221, Organizational Theory; 261, Policy Analysis in Public Administration; 373, American Political and Social Institutions; 374, Trends in Administrative Theory; 377, Social Action and Public Policy. (See also PAd. 264, Program Evaluation, under analytical methods.)

Evaluation Process

1. Paper submitted for publication (with scope and depth similar to lead articles in *Atlantic Monthly*) which critically presents a contemporary organizational, managerial, and/or policy debate.
2. Oral examination in which candidate will comprehensively respond to two case study questions and engage in discussion with supporting field adviser, an additional public administration professor, and attending students. The questions will be collaboratively developed by the candidate and adviser and will consist of two complex cases which pose problems similar to types of consulting experiences sought by the candidate. Previous to the examination, candidate will research information germane to theoretical issues, practical dilemmas, and policy questions embodied in the case study questions.

Additional Information

The general organization of the learning activities for this study plan is as follows. The first year was for orientation into the program, introduction to faculty and students, and validation of the fit between the program and my goals.

Even though I have courses from several areas in each of the following years of the program, I consider the thrust of the second year as my business background, the third year as my focus on organizational behavior and development, and the fourth year as my concentration on public administration.

The basic plan for each fall and spring semester is to have a variety of learning activities. I have usually included one theoretical course, one analytic course, one independent study, an experiential interpersonal learning, and an opportunity for practical consulting experience.

If my husband and I decide to have children, I will seek assistance from selected faculty and students on suggestions for anticipating and dealing with how that decision may impact on my study plan.

VII
Summary of Relationship Between Goals and Activities

Goal:	To be a university professor.	Proposed activities: Mgt. 390, 311–312, Soc. 241, Mgt. 205, 216, 398a, b, PAd. 221, 373, 261, 374, 377.
Goal:	To be a facilitator of learning.	Myers-Briggs Professional Qualifying Program, Mgt. 398c.
Goal:	To be a successful consultant.	Acct. 201, BAd. 246, PAd. 264, independent study with Gordon Lippitt, Mgt. 215, NTL and A. K. Rice group relations conferences, professional association meetings, consulting experiences.
Goal:	To be competent in research.	PAd. 296, 264, 374, Educ. 180, 282, Mgt. 391.
Goal:	To communicate effectively.	Mgt. 701, workbook on groups, Mgt. 398a, comprehensive evaluation activities.
Goal:	To work on my "Jablonski."	Group relations conferences, Mgt. 398a, c, feedback from advisers and colleagues, consulting experiences, taking and surviving risks, living.

Other Activities

Brief Identification	Method of Certifying Completion
Independent study with Gordon Lippitt on consultation and conflict management (fall 1984).	Written evaluation by self and professor using *Learning Event Analysis*.
Participation in group relations conferences (for example, NTL, A. K. Rice).	Certificates of attendance.
Attendance at professional meetings (for example, OD Network, AOTA, ASPA).	Copy of application receipt.
Consulting experiences (current and new positions).	Written feedback from supervising consultants and/or clients.
Completion of Myers-Briggs Professional Qualifying Program (spring 1985).	Certificate of completion.
Completion of workbook on leading groups in occupational therapy.	Submitted to publisher and contract encouragement.

Evaluative Processes

Process	Method of Certifying Completion
Oral presentation and discussion of a course proposal in major field. (Explained further in sections IV and V.)	Evaluation by major field adviser and additional professor and students in OBD.
Completion of in-depth article in public administration.	Submitted for publication after approval by supporting field adviser.
Oral examination on two case study questions in public administration.	Evaluation by supporting field adviser and additional professor and students in PAd.

Observations and Reflections

In the early days of experimentation with nontraditional degree programs, they were viewed with skepticism by traditional educators, the public, and the accrediting agencies. How could quality education and academic standards be assured if the learners were given so much freedom and if teachers were not in daily control of their studies? If there was no uniform curriculum? If there were no set requirements— or if the requirements could be negotiated away? If learners did not have immediate access to university libraries? If learners did not have the stimulation of daily interaction with one another?

No doubt in those early days there were instances of poor quality of learning and low academic standards. But as nontraditional institutions gained experience, they found solutions to these problems, and their graduates began demonstrating that they had indeed obtained an excellent education. Accreditation agencies began not only approving external degree programs but encouraging traditional institutions to offer them.

The selections in this chapter describe the procedures used by these institutions to assure quality educational outcomes. The principal tool, of course, is the degree contract, which makes visible to all parties concerned—learners, faculty members, resource people, and administrators—what learning objectives will be achieved and how, and how learning outcomes will be evaluated. The degree contracts vary in format but contain essentially the same information. I find that the Fielding Institute format provides the most detailed information.

All programs provide for some kind of orientational experience to prepare the learners to take the degree of responsibility this approach requires—the Fielding Institute through its Admissions and Contract Workshop, Metropolitan State University through its Individualized Educational Planning course, and the other programs through the services of advisers or mentors. And all of them provide printed guidelines.

The selection that is most questionable in this set is the George Washington University program, since it consists mainly of a set of courses. But I include it because it demonstrates that even a set of courses can be made more relevant to the goals of learners and can be organized into a developmental sequence that causes the courses to be seen as parts of a coherent whole rather than isolated fragments. When I think of all the courses I have taken in my long academic career, I can name only a few that I entered into with any understanding of how they would fit into a coherent whole program of personal and professional development. I took them to earn credits toward a degree. I saw myself as a "course taker" and "credit earner" rather than as a purposeful, goal-directed learner. I wish I had had the George Washington Study Plan process available to me.

NINE

Practical Hints on Achieving
Success with Contract Learning

About the Utility of Contract Learning

■ *The single most striking conclusion that can be drawn from the selections in this book about the utility of contract learning is that it is adaptable to a wide variety of situations. These selections describe its successful use in independent study, undergraduate and graduate academic and professional school courses, clinical placements and internships, continuing professional and management development, and total degree programs. They demonstrate that it yields many benefits but has some limitations, as listed in Chapter Two.*

About the Effectiveness of Contract Learning

Contract learning is such a recent development that not much empirical research has yet been done on it. One of the earliest studies, a survey of over 250 Empire State University students by Chickering (Berte, 1975, pp. 34–39), found that 46 percent evaluated the learning contract as superior to traditional methods, 26 percent rated it as "somewhat better," 13 percent as "comparable," and only 2 percent as "somewhat inferior." When students were asked to list the major weaknesses, 24 percent wrote "no weaknesses," 15 percent were bothered by the lack of group exchange, 10 percent mentioned the need for self-discipline, and 8 percent felt that they were too dependent on one mentor.

Another study, by Caffarella (1983, pp. 7–26), reporting on fifty-four students' evaluations of the experience of using learning contracts in graduate courses, reached three conclusions:

1. *That using a learning contract format in graduate courses is worthwhile and valuable and that it should be continued in graduate-level courses.*
2. *That the students had increased their competencies as self-directed learners as a result of using the learning contract.*
3. *That they were using the competencies they had gained from the process in their current teaching situations and personal learning experiences, both at home and at work.*

Morris T. Keeton, president of the Council for Adult and Experiential Education, made an independent evaluation of the College Without Walls at Sinclair Community College in Dayton, Ohio (see Selection 8), in 1980 and found the following outcomes as reported in interviews:

1. *More effective integration of theory and practice.*
2. *Greater sense of ownership for one's learning.*
3. *Increased ability to define and set measurable goals.*
4. *Enhanced self-concept.*
5. *Greater self-motivation to learn, participate, and achieve.*
6. *More realistic attitudes toward work and careers.*
7. *Enhanced awareness of individual strengths and weaknesses (Cowperthwaite, n.d., pp. 22–23).*

Selection 3 reports the positive findings of the evaluation of use of learning contracts in clinical nursing placement by both learners and preceptors at Capital University.

If the descriptions and sentiments presented in the selections in this book can be considered action research, we must conclude that contract learning has been shown to be an effective mode of education in a wide variety of situations.

About the Process of Contract Learning

An analysis of the selections in this book suggests that three critical variables affect the success of contract learning: institutional support, preparation of the learners, and preparation of the faculty.

Institutional Support. Many of the selections in this book are from nontraditional institutions where support for innovative approaches to education is integral to the philosophy of the institutions. But in traditional institutions policy makers may be reluctant to support contract learning, fearing that it will result in loss of control, accountability, and academic standards. I hope that the case examples presented here will give innovators who want to experiment with contract learning ammunition for convincing their colleagues that the process has been used in a variety of institutions without any of these losses.

Strategies for introducing contract learning into a system are described in Chapter Three.

Preparation of Learners. It is predictable that, when first exposed to the idea of contract learning, many learners will react with confusion, resistance, and anxiety. After all, for most of them their only previous experience with education has been with the teacher making all the decisions about what they will learn, how they will learn it, when they will learn it, and whether they have learned it. Few of them have been allowed, much less invited, to participate in making decisions about their learning. It is a strange and scary prospect, hence the importance of providing a preparatory experience that will help them become more confident about their ability to take some responsibility for planning, carrying out, and evaluating their own learning. Several strategies for doing this are described in the selections in this book.

Probably the most common strategy is providing the learners with clear guidelines for engaging in this process. Chapter One presents an example of a set of generic guidelines. More situation-specific guidelines can be found in Selections 5, 7, 14, 16, and 22.

A more intensive preparation is accomplished by workshops or seminars designed specifically to acquaint learners with the concept and process of contract learning and engage them in skill-practice exercises in drafting contracts. Examples of this strategy are presented in Selections 20 and 21.

Another strategy, described in Selections 2 and 3, is to start by having the learners draft a contract for a small unit of a learning experience and then increasing the units incrementally.

Selections 7, 8, 17, 18, and 20 describe the use of an advisory committee, multiple sponsors, or a peer support group for guiding learners through the process.

Some of the selections explain how they provide learners with sample contracts drafted by previous learners. The first time I experimented with this strategy, I distributed only one sample contract and got back from the learners pretty much a carbon copy of that sample. I learned fast to distribute three or four examples quite different from one another. I hope that this book will be used as a resource for learners (and faculty members) to examine a variety of examples of contracts.

Preparation of Faculty. In order for contract learning as presented in this book to work well, instructors and mentors must accomplish a transformation of their roles and strategies in at least the following respects.

First, they must reorient their perception of their role away from that of the traditional controller of learners and transmitter of content toward that of a facilitator of self-directed learners. This shift involves a redefinition of their roles as serving primarily as designers and managers of procedures for helping learners acquire the content and only secondarily as content resources. Of course, they have a responsibility to make available to learners whatever content resources they possess, but even more important, they have a responsibility to keep informed about other content resources, both human and material, with which they can link learners. I perceive, for example, that one of the most important functions I perform as a facilitator of learning is serving as an educational broker—a linker of learners with the most effective resources for acquiring particular kinds of knowledge, skills, attitudes, and values. I make a point of keeping up-to-date information about the growing body of material resources—books, articles, audiovisual materials, multimedia learning packages, computer-based programs, and the like—as well as about people with specialized information and skills. I also perceive my role to be that of colearner, engaging in a process of shared inquiry with those whose learning I am trying to facilitate. In fact, I can state unequivocally that over the years I have learned more from and with my students than from all the teachers I have studied under combined.

Second, faculty members must change their psychic reward system from valuing the extent to which the learners conform to their direction to valuing the extent to which the learners take the initiative in directing their own learning. Traditional teachers tend to get satisfaction from controlling the energy of learners; facilitators get their satisfaction from releasing the energy of learners. I can testify, as can the authors of the selections in this book, that it is a joyful moment for a facilitator when learners become excited and energized in carrying out their self-planned learning contracts.

Third, instructors and mentors must develop a different set of skills that are more associated with the role of counselor or consultant than with that of didactic teacher. In this regard, I have found Carl Rogers's (1969) three characteristics of an effective helper to be especially useful: (1) unqualified positive regard for the client or learner as a valued person, (2) a deep ability to empathize—to listen carefully so as to understand the learners' thoughts and feel their feelings, and (3) absolute authenticity—behaving as the real you (not role-playing being a professor). But some technical skills are involved as well, such as skill in designing and managing learning experiences that will help learners acquire the attitudes and skills of self-directed learning (Knowles, 1975, pp. 31–58).

The question in most readers' minds at this point is probably "How do you help faculty members modify their role definitions and acquire these attitudes and skills?" I have been impressed over and over by the reports I have received from teachers around the world who describe how they have modified their practice simply as a result of reading books and articles on self-directed and contract learning. My hypothesis is that early in the experience of working with adults many teachers become dissatisfied with the results of the traditional pedagogical approach and become ready to investigate new approaches. In fact, my faith in this hypothesis was my chief motivation for preparing this book.

A more intensive and systematic strategy is to engage faculty members in a learning activity in which they experience the contracting process themselves and then analyze it. Since my retirement from North Carolina State University in 1979, for example, I have conducted an average of thirty or more one- or two-day workshops for faculties each year and have been impressed with how much behavioral change takes place in even so short a time. Many of the selections in this book, in fact, are the result of their authors' having attended one of my workshops. The process design I use in these workshops is described in Knowles (1980), p. 322. I believe that the reason it is successful is that it first puts the participants in the role of adult learners; they diagnose their own learning needs as facilitators of learning (using the self-diagnostic rating scale in Chapter One) and draft a learning contract to accomplish the objectives derived from their learning needs. They experience what it is like to be treated as an adult learner, and they experience the excitement of participating in planning and carrying out their own learning. Then we analyze this experience together to identify the attitudes and skills involved in facilitating self-directed learners and to explore the theoretical framework (andragogy) on which this approach is based.

No doubt there are teachers who are so talented as didactic instructors that they have no interest in investigating a different approach and should not be pressured into it. But it has been my experience that a great number of instructors around the country and, indeed, around the world are hungry for new approaches that work better with adult learners. It is to them that this book is dedicated.

References

Aldridge, H. "Student Contracts." Speech presented at the Long Beach Conference for Foreign Language Framework, Long Beach, Calif., 1971. ERIC Document Reproduction Service No. ED 055 503.

Avakian, A. P. "Writing a Learning Contract." In D. W. Vermilye (ed.), *Lifelong Learners: A New Clientele for Higher Education.* San Francisco: Jossey-Bass, 1974.

Banathy, B. H. *Instructional Systems.* Palo Alto, Calif.: Fearon, 1968.

Barlow, R. M. "An Experiment with Learning Contracts." *Journal of Higher Education,* 1974, *45,* 441–450.

Baskin, S. "Independent Study Methods, Programs, and for Whom?" In G. K. Smith (ed.), *Current Issues in Higher Education.* Washington, D.C.: Association for Higher Education, 1962.

Baughart, F. W. *Educational Systems Analysis.* New York: Macmillan, 1969.

Bertalanffy, L. V. *General Systems Theory.* New York: Braziller, 1963.

Berte, N. R. (ed.). *Individualizing Education by Learning Contracts.* New Directions for Higher Education, no. 10. San Francisco: Jossey-Bass, 1975.

Bloom, B. S. "Learning for Mastery." In *Evaluation Comment.* Los Angeles: Center for the Study of Evaluation of Instructional Programs, University of California, 1968.

Boshier, R. *Towards a Learning Society*. Vancouver: Learning-press, 1980.

Botkin, J. W., Elmandjra, M., and Malitza, M. *No Limits to Learning: A Report to the Club of Rome*. Elmsford, N.Y.: Pergamon Press, 1979.

Boud, D. *Developing Student Autonomy in Learning*. New York: Nichols, 1981.

Boyd, E. M. "Contract Learning." *Physical Therapy*, 1979, *59*, 278-281.

Burke, J. D., and others. *Teaching History via Learning Contracts*. Buffalo: State University of New York–Buffalo, 1977.

Bushnell, D., and Rappaport, D. (eds.). *Planned Change in Education: A Systems Approach*. San Diego, Calif.: Harcourt Brace Jovanovich, 1972.

Caffarella, R. S. "The Learning Plan Format: A Technique for Incorporating the Concept of Learning How to Learn into Formal Courses and Workshops." In *Proceedings: Lifelong Learning Research Conference*, University of Maryland, College Park, Feb. 12-13, 1982.

Caffarella, R. S. "Fostering Self-Directed Learning in Post-Secondary Education: The Use of Learning Contracts." *Lifelong Learning*, 1983, 7(3), 7-26.

Carnegie Foundation for the Advancement of Teaching. *Missions of the College Curriculum: A Contemporary Review with Suggestions*. San Francisco: Jossey-Bass, 1977.

Charland, W. A., Jr. "Individualized Education with Adults: Some Principles and Practical Advice." *Alternative Higher Education: The Journal of Nontraditional Studies*, 1980, 5(2), 121-125.

Chickering, A. W. *Education and Identity*. San Francisco: Jossey-Bass, 1969.

Chickering, A. W., and Associates. *The Modern American College: Responding to the New Realities of Diverse Students and a Changing Society*. San Francisco: Jossey-Bass, 1981.

Commission on Non-Traditional Study. *Diversity by Design*. San Francisco: Jossey-Bass, 1973.

Cook, J. M. *Developing Program Maps*. Columbia, Md.: Council for the Advancement of Experiential Learning, 1978.

Cowperthwaite, G. "Individualized Education Is Alive and Doing Well." Unpublished document, College Without Walls, Sinclair Community College, Dayton, Ohio, n.d.

Cowperthwaite, G. "Options for Lifelong Learners: The External Degree." In B. Heermann, C. C. Enders, and E. Wine (eds.), *Serving Lifelong Learners*. New Directions for Community Colleges, no. 29. San Francisco: Jossey-Bass, 1980.

Cropley, A. J. (ed.). *Towards a System of Lifelong Learning.* Hamburg, Germany: UNESCO Institute for Education, 1980.

Cross, K. P. *Accent on Learning: Improving Instruction and Reshaping the Curriculum.* San Francisco: Jossey-Bass, 1976.

Cross, K. P. *The Missing Link: Connecting Adult Learners to Learning Resources.* Princeton, N.J.: College Board Publications, 1979.

Cross, K. P. *Adults as Learners: Increasing Participation and Facilitating Learning.* San Francisco: Jossey-Bass, 1981.

Dave, R. H. *Reflections on Lifelong Learning and the School.* Hamburg, Germany: UNESCO Institute for Education, 1975.

Donovan, M., Wolpert, P., and Yacho, J. "Gaps and Contracts." *Nursing Outlook,* Aug. 1981, pp. 467–471.

Dressel, P. L. (ed.). *The New Colleges: Toward an Appraisal.* Iowa City, Iowa: American College Testing Program, 1971.

Dressel, P. L., and Thompson, M. M. *Independent Study: New Interpretations of Concepts, Practices, and Problems.* San Francisco: Jossey-Bass, 1973.

Duley, J. "Out-of-Class Contract Learning at Justin Morrill." *New Directions in Higher Education,* 1975, *3,* 53–63.

Dunn, R., and Dunn, K. *Practical Approaches to Individualizing Instruction: Contracts and Other Effective Teaching Strategies.* West Nyack, N.Y.: Parker, 1975.

Egan, G., and Cowan, M. A. *People in Systems: A Model for Development in Human-Service Professions and Education.* Monterey, Calif.: Brooks/Cole, 1979.

Fairchild, R. P. *Person-Centered Graduate Education.* Buffalo, N.Y.: Prometheus Books, 1977.

Faure, E., and others. *Learning to Be.* Paris: UNESCO, 1972.

Gibbs, G. *Learning to Study: A Guide to Running Group Sessions.* Milton Keynes, U.K.: British Open University, 1977.

Gould, S. B., and Cross, K. P. (eds.). *Explorations in Non-Traditional Study*. San Francisco: Jossey-Bass, 1972.

Gross, R. *The Lifelong Learner*. New York: Simon & Schuster, 1977.

Gruber, H. E., and Weitman, M. *Self-Directed Study: Experiments in Higher Education*. Boulder: University of Colorado, 1962.

Hartley, H. J. *Educational Planning-Programming-Budgeting: A Systems Approach*. Englewood Cliffs, N.J.: Prentice-Hall, 1968.

Heffernan, J. M., and others. *Educational Brokering: A New Service for Adult Learners*. Washington, D.C.: National Center for Educational Brokering, 1976.

Hiemstra, R. (ed.). "Policy Recommendations Related to Self-Directed Learning." Occasional paper no. 1, Syracuse University, 1980.

Homme, L., and others. *How to Use Contingency Contracting in the Classroom*. Champaign, Ill.: Research Press, 1970.

Houle, C. O. *The Inquiring Mind*. Madison: University of Wisconsin Press, 1961.

Houle, C. O. *The Design of Education*. San Francisco: Jossey-Bass, 1972.

Houle, C. O. *The External Degree*. San Francisco: Jossey-Bass, 1973.

Houle, C. O. *Continuing Learning in the Professions*. San Francisco: Jossey-Bass, 1980.

Ingalls, J. D., and Arceri, J. M. *A Trainers' Guide to Andragogy*. SRS 72-05301. U.S. Department of Health, Education and Welfare. Washington, D.C.: U.S. Government Printing Office, 1972.

Kaufman, R. *Educational System Planning*. Englewood Cliffs, N.J.: Prentice-Hall, 1972.

Kautzmann, L. "A Model for Teaching Group Dynamics to Occupational Therapy Students." Ed.D. practicum paper, Nova University, 1984.

Keeton, M. T., and Associates. *Experiential Learning: Rationale, Characteristics, and Assessment*. San Francisco: Jossey-Bass, 1976.

Keeton, M. T., and Tate, P. J. "A Boom in Experiential Learning." In M. T. Keeton and P. J. Tate (eds.), *Learning By*

Experience—What, Why, How. New Directions for Experiential Learning, no. 1, San Francisco: Jossey-Bass, 1978.

Kelly, G. S. *The Psychology of Personal Constructs.* New York: Norton, 1955.

Kerwin, M. "Andragogy in the Community College." *Community College Review,* 1981, *9*(3), 12–14.

Kidd, J. R. *How Adults Learn.* New York: Cambridge University Press, 1973.

Kimizuka, S. "Preparing Learning Activity Packets for Individual Instruction: Student Contracts Approach." ERIC Document Reproduction Service No. ED 081 284.

Knowles, M. S. *Higher Adult Education in the United States.* Washington, D.C.: American Council on Education, 1969.

Knowles, M. S. *Self-Directed Learning: A Guide for Learners and Teachers.* New York: Cambridge Book Company, 1975.

Knowles, M. S. *The Modern Practice of Adult Education: From Pedagogy to Andragogy.* (2nd ed.) New York: Cambridge Book Company, 1980.

Knowles, M. S. *The Adult Learner: A Neglected Species.* (3rd ed.) Houston: Gulf, 1984.

Knowles, M. S. "Shifting to an HRD Systems Approach." *Training and Development Journal,* 1985, *39*(5), 24–25.

Knowles, M. S., and Associates. *Andragogy in Action: Applying Modern Principles of Adult Learning.* San Francisco: Jossey-Bass, 1984.

Kolb, D. A. "Learning Styles and Disciplinary Differences." In A. W. Chickering and Associates, *The Modern American College.* San Francisco: Jossey-Bass, 1981.

Lavery, J. W. "The Learning Contract in Adult Education and Lifelong Learning." Paper presented at Lifelong Learning Research Conference, University of Maryland, College Park, Feb. 6–7, 1981.

Lehman, T. "Evaluating Contract Learning." In D. W. Vermilye (ed.), *Learner-Centered Reform.* San Francisco: Jossey-Bass, 1975.

Lindquist, J. "Strategies for Contract Learning." In D. W. Vermilye (ed.), *Learner-Centered Reform.* San Francisco: Jossey-Bass, 1975.

McKeachie, W. J. "Research in Teaching at the College and University Level." In N. L. Gage (ed.), *Handbook of Research on Teaching*. Skokie, Ill.: Rand McNally, 1963.

Mayville, W. "Contract Learning." *ERIC Higher Education Research Currents*, Dec. 1973.

Meyer, P. *Awarding College Credit for Non-College Learning: A Guide to Current Practices*. San Francisco: Jossey-Bass, 1975.

Milton, O. *Alternatives to the Traditional: How Professors Teach and How Students Learn*. San Francisco: Jossey-Bass, 1972.

Milton, O., and Associates. *On College Teaching: A Guide to Contemporary Practices*. San Francisco: Jossey-Bass, 1978.

Minter, J. W. (ed.). *The Individual and the System*. Boulder, Colo.: Western Interstate Commission for Higher Education, 1967.

Newcomb, L. H., and Warsbrod, R. J. "The Effect of Contract Grading on Student Performance." ERIC Document Reproduction Service No. ED 093 967.

Newman, F. *Report on Higher Education*. Washington, D.C.: U.S. Government Printing Office, 1971.

Perry, W. *The Open University: History and Evaluation of a Dynamic Innovation in Higher Education*. San Francisco: Jossey-Bass, 1977.

Pfeiffer, J. *A New Look at Education: Systems Analysis in Schools and Colleges*. New York: Odyssey, 1968.

Rogers, C. R. *Freedom to Learn*. Columbus, Ohio: Merrill, 1969.

Runkel, P., and others. *The Changing College Classroom*. San Francisco: Jossey-Bass, 1969.

Rust, V. D. *Alternatives in Education: Historical and Theoretical Perspectives*. Beverly Hills, Calif.: Sage, 1977.

Schluster, J. "Effects of Performance Contracting on Students in Settings of Higher Education." Unpublished manuscript, Syracuse University, 1979.

Schuttenberg, E. M., and Poppenhagen, B. W. *Field Experiences in Postsecondary Education: A Guidebook for Action*. Lanham, Md.: University Press of America, 1980.

Siegel, L. "The Contributions and Implications of Recent Research Related to Improving Teaching and Learning." In O. Milton and E. J. Shoben, Jr. (eds.), *Learning and the Professors*. Athens: Ohio University Press, 1968.

Smith, R. M. *Learning How to Learn: Applied Theory for Adults.* New York: Cambridge Book Company, 1982.

Stein, L. S. *Your Personal Learning Plan: A Handbook for Physicians.* Chicago: Illinois Council on Continuing Medical Education, 1973.

Sullivan, E. (ed.). *Guide to External Degree Programs in the United States.* (2nd ed.) New York: Macmillan, 1983.

Tenore, E. J., and Dunbar, S. E. *One Step Beyond: A Systems Approach to Delivering Individualized Instruction.* Pittsfield, Mass.: Berkshire Community Press, 1979.

Tough, A. *Learning Without a Teacher.* Toronto: Ontario Institute for Studies in Education, 1967.

Tough, A. *The Adult's Learning Projects.* Toronto: Ontario Institute for Studies in Education, 1979.

Vermilye, D. W. (ed.). *The Expanded Campus.* San Francisco: Jossey-Bass, 1972.

Vermilye, D. W. (ed.). *Lifelong Learners: A New Clientele for Higher Education.* San Francisco: Jossey-Bass, 1974.

Vermilye, D. W. (ed.). *Learner-Centered Reform.* San Francisco: Jossey-Bass, 1975.

Weinstock, C. *Learning Contracts: Facilitating Academic Change.* Seattle: Washington State Board for Community College Education, 1973. ERIC Document Reproduction Service No. ED 080 107.

Zalatimo, S. D., and Sleeman, P. J. *A Systems Approach to Learning Environments.* Roselle, N.J.: MEDED Project, 1975.

Index